THE *Oster* KITCHEN CENTER®
FOOD PREPARATION APPLIANCE
BRAND
COOKBOOK

A Benjamin Company Book

Editor:	Sherrill Weary
Production Assistants:	Helen Geist
	Pat Drew
	Susan Jablonski
Chief Home Economist:	Betty Sullivan
Consulting Home Economists:	Mary Beth Jung
	Wendy Wieser Spinelli
	Mary Hanneman
	Alice Pearson
	Dora Jonassen
Art & Design:	Thomas C. Brecklin
Typography:	A-Line, Milwaukee
Photography:	Walter Storck

®Oster, Osterizer, Kitchen Center, Mini-Blend,
™FoodCrafter, Power Purée 'N Ricer

Library of Congress Catalog Card Number: 80-70443
ISBN: 0-87502-086-0
Published by The Benjamin Company, Inc.
One Westchester Plaza
Elmsford, New York 10523
10 9 8 7 6 5 4 3 2

Welcome!

This book is dedicated to you, the owner of the Oster "Kitchen Center" appliance. We know you purchased this appliance to assist in preparing creative, nutritious and economical meals for every day and special company occasions.

Oster has long believed in aiding the consumer by developing time saving and labor saving appliances. As far back as 1924 John Oster in Racine, Wisconsin, pioneered the development of the first hand-held hair clipper.

The famous "Osterizer" blender soon followed and was the original electric food preparation machine. Its introduction in 1946 started a revolution in food and beverage preparation in the home. A revolution that would be the foundation from which other quality products such as the Oster "Kitchen Center" brand food preparation appliance would evolve.

The Oster "Kitchen Center" Cookbook includes many pages of "how-to" pictures and operational tips to save you time and money during recipe preparation. The kitchen-tested recipes that follow are geared to work with your "Kitchen Center" appliance to eliminate tedious, old-fashioned kitchen tasks. Just think, you'll never have to hand shred carrots for salad, or potatoes for hash browns again! Let your Oster "Kitchen Center" appliance do the work for you.

So sit back with your new cookbook and browse through the many chapters of tempting recipes and beautiful pictures. We know you'll find just the right recipe for every occasion. We also know you'll love the ease of food preparation with your Oster "Kitchen Center" appliance.

Bon Appetit!

Mary Beth Jung, Director
Home Economics Department

Let's Get Acquainted

Meet the machine that chops, blends, slices, shreds, grinds, crumbs, kneads, mixes and more — The Oster "Kitchen Center" brand food preparation appliance. The machine is 5 appliances in one — a mixer, blender, doughmaker, grinder and saladmaker.

The electronically controlled mixer has an infinite number of speeds, allowing you to fold in the lightest of ingredients yet mix the heaviest of batters. Use the famous "Osterizer" blender to chop vegetables, nuts, and cheese, to make baby food, frosting, mayonnaise and of course, to blend your favorite beverages. The doughmaker is a powerful work horse which kneads dough with up to 7 cups (1.75 liters) of flour in just 7 minutes. Imagine — no more hand kneading! Grind your own hamburger, cracker crumbs, nuts, cheese, sandwich spreads and more with the powerful food grinder. The saladmaker quickly slices, shreds, chops, crumbs and french fry cuts fruits,

vegetables, cheeses, crackers and more with continuous feeding action. Your "Kitchen Center" appliance will save you time and money in food preparation.

Use the beginning section of this cookbook to learn the basic techniques for using your "Kitchen Center" appliance. Once you have mastered these techniques, your imagination is the only limit in preparing all of your favorite recipes using your Oster "Kitchen Center" appliance.

"KITCHEN CENTER" BLENDER

The "Osterizer" blender can speed up food preparation by chopping, grinding, grating, liquefying and crumbing.

The blender processes food by using two basic methods. These methods are outlined in the labeled pictures on the following pages. Try these techniques and apply them to your favorite recipes for easier food preparation.

BLENDER CHOPPING

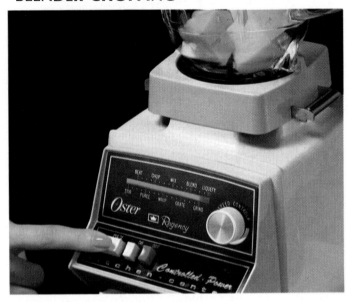

PULSE *The PULSE, ON and OFF buttons, on the Motor Base are used to control all actions of the blender. The Pulse button enables you to quickly start and stop the blender in an ON/OFF action. This type of blending action allows you to precisely control the texture of the food being processed. This type of operation is called "Controlled Cycle Blending" in your instruction book.*

To PULSE, simply depress and release the Pulse button at 2-second intervals. The recipes in this book refer to this time period as a CYCLE. A CYCLE is 2 seconds (counting 1001, 1002). Allow blades to stop before pulsing again. The more cycles used, the finer the end product texture will be.

DRY CHOP VEGETABLES-small quantities

Vegetables such as onions, carrots and green peppers can be chopped in the blender in small quantities. Put only 1 cup (250 ml) of 1" (2.5 cm) cubes of vegetables into the container. Cover container. Pulse (see photo #1) the number of cycles needed to get desired results. This method is called **dry chop**. *If more than 1 cup (250 ml) is needed, follow procedure for* **water chop**, *page 11.*

BLENDER CHOPPED CHEESE *Cheese should be refrigerator cold. Mozzarella, Swiss, Parmesan, Cheddar and others can be processed in the blender. Do not process more than 1 cup (250 ml) of cubes at a time.*

DRIED FRUITS *Dates and dried fruits can also be chopped. Measure 1/2 cup (125 ml) candied fruit or date pieces and mix with 1/2 cup (125 ml) flour. (Flour can be measured from amount called for in recipe.) Put into container. Cover and process 2-3 cycles at LIQUEFY or until desired texture is reached.*

DRAINING *Immediately after processing, empty contents of blender container into colander to drain off liquid. If desired, use water for soup stock.*

WATER CHOPPING - large quantities *Large quantities of food can be chopped in the blender by adding a liquid. Water (or any liquid) will circulate the food through the blades so all food will be chopped. Place up to 5 cups (1.25 liters) of 1" (2.5 cm) cubes into blender container. Cover with cold water. Cover with lid and process number of cycles needed to get desired results. For coleslaw process 3 cycles at GRIND.*

VARIATION TO WATER CHOPPING *Your favorite recipe that calls for chopped vegetables can be converted to use with the blender. Instead of water, put liquid ingredients from recipe into the blender container and add pieces of food to be chopped. Cover and process the number of cycles needed to achieve desired results. Do not drain away the liquid. For example, Chili can be prepared quickly by placing green pepper and onion into container with tomato sauce. Cover and pulse number of cycles needed to get desired results.*

CONTINUOUS BLENDING

CONTINUOUS BLENDING *Peanut butter, mayonnaise, dressings and pancakes use a continuous blending action that produces a smooth-textured end product. Use the ON and OFF buttons to control the blender action. Always put liquid ingredients first into blender container. If mixture is too thick, more liquid may need to be added so proper circulation (whirlpool) can occur. It may be necessary with some mixtures to use a rubber spatula. To properly use rubber spatula, turn the blender off and move mixture into processing blades with rubber spatula.*

BLENDER GRINDING *Whole grains, coffee beans and spices can be ground in the blender. Place 1 cup (250 ml) into blender container. Cover and process at GRIND until desired texture is reached. The longer the processing, the finer the texture. Pictured: Whole wheat grain in blender, cracked wheat (left), whole wheat flour (right).*

BLENDER CRUMBING *Different textures can be achieved by using various techniques. The combination of higher speeds and number of cycles can produce coarse (1 cycle at STIR) or medium (2 cycles at GRATE) crumbs. Fine crumbs are produced by running the blender continuously at GRIND. Simply push the ON button. Allow the motor to run until the bread is finely crumbed. Push OFF button to shut unit off. Crackers, cookies and wafers can be crumbed using these two techniques.*

LIQUEFYING ICE *Add ice for beverages through feeder cap opening while processing at LIQUEFY. Whenever processing ice, be sure to have at least 1 cup (250 ml) liquid in blender container.*

FEEDER CAP *Remove feeder cap from cover to add ingredients while blending food while the motor is running. This allows food to be completely mixed as in dressings and mayonnaise.*

GRATING *Hard foods such as fresh coconut and cheese can be grated. Cover and turn motor to BLEND. With motor running, remove feeder cap and drop no more than 1 cup (250 ml) of 1" (2.5 cm) cubes into container. Turn blender OFF.*

Cooked meats can also be processed, using same techniques, to produce chopped meats for sandwich spreads. Hard dried out cheeses can also be used. Cheese should always be refrigerator cold for best results.

REMOVING MIXTURES

THICK MIXTURES *Thick mixtures can be removed from bottom of blender. Remove blade assembly and scrape mixture from sides of blender. This will also make cleaning the container easier.*

"MINI-BLEND" ACCESSORY (8-ounce or 250 ml) *Small quantities of 1/2 cup (125 ml) can be chopped and then stored in the 8-ounce (250 ml) "Mini-Blend" container. The "Mini-Blend" container is perfect for processing onions, bread crumbs, parsley, peppercorns and coffee beans.*

THIN MIXTURES *The pouring lip allows thinner mixtures to be poured directly from blender container. Pancakes are processed, then poured directly onto hot griddle.*

"KITCHEN CENTER" SALAD MAKER

The "FoodCrafter" slicer/shredder/salad maker is designed to save you time. You can slice, shred, crumb, julienne, and more in seconds. Each slice is perfectly cut with more precision and in less time than you ever thought possible.

The pages that follow in this section will show you the variety of foods typically processed with your basic and accessory cutting discs. You will be delighted to see how many time-consuming tasks you can let your Oster "Kitchen Center" appliance do for you.

Besides saving time, your unit will slice dollars off your food budget. Many of the costly convenience foods you now purchase can be prepared at home quickly with greater nutritional advantages.

Learn the basic techniques shown here and you will be able to prepare all your favorite recipes with ease. Be sure to consult your instruction book that came with your appliance for assembly and specific processing speeds for your unit.

LOADING FOOD HOPPER

Correct loading of Food Hopper will insure precision cuts for your fruits and vegetables. For many foods that will be used in casseroles and soups it is not as important to have perfect slices. But, when it is important, be sure to follow the directions below and on page 16.

DISCHARGE CHUTE *The Discharge Chute allows for processing large or small quantities or precision-cut ingredients. It is especially designed to make quick work when processing fruits and vegetables for canning and freezing. Use your 4-quart (4 liter) mixer bowl to catch your ingredients.*

LARGE PUSHER *To insure perfect slices, especially with long narrow foods, firmly pack Hopper. Cut all foods approximately the same length and slightly shorter than Hopper height. Push food down into Disc with even pressure on Larger Pusher. Follow this technique for celery, cucumbers, zucchini, etc.*

Perfect slices are achieved by making sure the foods are positioned correctly and firmly packed in the Hopper. When a small quantity is to be processed, such as one rib of celery, use the Split Pushers as shown.

If your model "Kitchen Center" appliance does not include Split Pushers, position single food in Hopper closest to you. Hold firmly in place with Large Pusher and turn unit on. The rotation of the Disc will push food against Hopper to hold it upright as it processes. Be sure both ends of food are flat to avoid tipping.

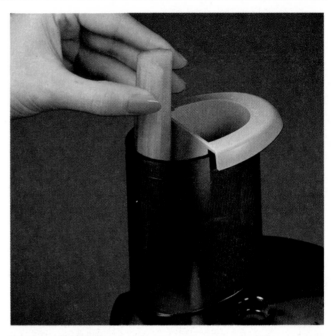

SMALL PUSHER *Use the Small Pusher when processing a single small vegetable such as celery, small zucchini or a carrot. Place Medium Pusher in Hopper on textured side and guide vegetable into Disc with Small Pusher.*

MEDIUM PUSHER *When processing a large single vegetable that does not completely fill the Hopper, place Small Pusher in Hopper on textured side. Place food into Hopper and feed into Disc with Medium Pusher.*

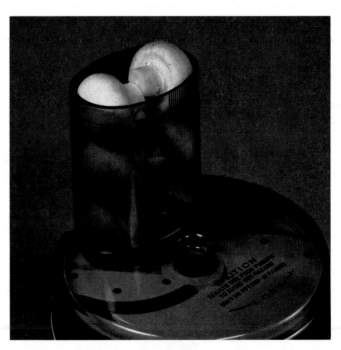

SPECIAL SLICING TECHNIQUES *When perfect slices are desired for small foods such as mushrooms, olives and strawberries, take special care when packing Hopper. For example, lay mushrooms on their sides in alternating patterns. Pack firmly. Use a gentle but even pressure on Pusher when processing to hold food in place.*

SHREDDER DISC

The time-consuming task of shredding vegetables and cheese, finely chopping nuts, crumbing bread, cookies and cracker crumbs, is past history. Shredded carrot salads, Zucchini Breads and Apple Cakes are now easier than ever to prepare.

SHREDDER DISC *With some foods the Shredder Disc will produce a fine texture. Process nuts for baking; eggs for salads, garnishes or spreads; and crackers for breading and crusts. Why not process large quantities of food right into plastic storage bags for use at a later date?.*

SHREDDER DISC *Use Shredder Disc to speed the tedious job of shredding large quantities of food. Process carrots, cheese (refrigerator-cold Mozzarella or Swiss), beets, and zucchini. Longer shreds may be obtained by laying food down horizontally in Hopper, if desired.*

WHITE SHREDDER DISC *(White Shredder Disc only) Process cranberries for relish, olives for appetizers, and cabbage for slaws and relishes. You'll also enjoy the finely minced texture of processed onions and green peppers for dips and spreads.*

THIN SLICER DISC

THIN SLICER DISC *Salads and Oriental dishes will be easier to prepare with the Thin Slicer Disc. Radishes, zucchini and water chestnuts can be sliced paper thin for maximum flavor and appearance. Pack zucchini into Hopper as shown on pages 15 and 16.*

THIN SLICER DISC *Mushrooms for salad and sautéeing; onions for salads and casseroles; potatoes for deep frying and creamed casseroles; all can be prepared with the Thin Slicer Disc. Position mushrooms and onions carefully as discussed on page 16.*

THIN SLICER DISC *Process red cabbage for vegetable side dishes; cabbage for slaw; carrots for tossed salads, molded vegetable salads, Oriental Dishes; cranberries for Holiday Breads. See page 16 for directions to properly pack carrots for slicing into Hopper.*

THICK SLICER DISC

THICK SLICER DISC *To make your own salad bar use the Thick Slicer Disc to process beets, lettuce and stuffed olives. Use all the Cutting Discs to prepare a wide variety of ingredients for your salad bar. Beets can also be prepared for canning using this Disc.*

THICK SLICER DISC *Use Thick Slicer Disc to process potatoes for frying and scalloped potatoes; peppers and onions for salads and casseroles. Carrots, celery, zucchini and cucumbers are also sliced with this Disc and can be used as dippers, in soups, stews and vegetable dishes. Careful placement of foods in Hopper will insure perfect slices. Onions should be placed root side down in Hopper. Peppers should be halved and firmly packed in Hopper before processing.*

THICK SLICER DISC *Your favorite pies and desserts can be prepared quickly when using your Thick Slicer Disc. Apples, bananas and pears are only three examples of fruits you can slice.*

Many fruits, such as peaches and strawberries, can be sliced for freezing with this Disc. Firmly pack Hopper with apple, peach or pear halves before processing for perfect slices.

FRENCH FRY CUTTER DISC

The French Fry Cutter Disc makes quick work of cutting raw potatoes for crisp French Fries. This versatile Disc can process many other foods to a coarsely chopped texture or into interesting julienne strips.

FRENCH FRY CUTTER *Use the French Fry Cutter to process potatoes, pared or unpared, for French Fries (recipe page 133); cooked beets for salads and vegetable side dishes; zucchini for Oriental Stir-Fry, salads and casseroles.*

FRENCH FRY CUTTER *A chopped effect can be produced with the French Fry Cutter when processing onions, celery, cabbage and green peppers. You will find these textures just right for casseroles, salads and soups. If coarsely chopped nuts are desired, this Disc can also be used.*

"FOODCRAFTER" ACCESSORY DISCS

To increase the versatility of your Salad Maker there are optional Accessory Discs available. The Chunky and Crinkle Cutting Discs will make food preparation both practical and fun.

CHUNKY CUTTER DISC *Use our Chunky Cutter Disc to process your favorite vegetables for soups, stews, casseroles, canning and freezing. The heftier cut is also great for vegetables served as appetizer dippers. Process zucchini, carrots and celery for starters in this practical Cutting Disc.*

CHUNKY CUTTER DISC *Fresh fruit salad and fruits prepared for freezing and canning are cut perfectly with the Chunky Cutter Disc. Its thicker cut is especially good for processing ripe fruits for pies and desserts.*

CRINKLE CUTTER DISC *When you want to add a decorative look to your foods, use the Crinkle Cutter Disc. Cut cucumbers, carrots and beets for salads, appetizer trays and vegetable side dishes. Canned and frozen foods will have more interest when crinkle cut. Potatoes and zucchini can also be processed.*

"KITCHEN CENTER" DOUGHMAKER

The Oster "Kitchen Center" dough-maker kneads dough with up to 7 cups (1.75 liters) of flour in just 7 minutes, making 2 beautiful 1 1/2-pound (651 g) loaves.

The following tips will help you bake beautiful loaves:

—Unless the dough is sticky, there is no need to flour the surface you are rolling on.

STEP 1 *Assemble doughmaker as directed in your instruction book. Heat the liquid for bread to 120°F (48°C) for all recipes in this book. Check the temperature with a thermometer. Combine half the flour and the remaining ingredients. Mix at the speed recommended in your instruction book.*

—Bread dough can rise in the oven in the following manner. Turn the oven on to the lowest setting for 10 minutes. Turn the oven off and place the dough in the oven. Gas ovens with pilot lights have enough heat without preheating the oven.

—Fill bread pans 1/3 to 1/2 full. Use dull aluminum pans, bread will not brown in shiny aluminum pans. If using glass pans, reduce oven temperature by 25°F (15°C).

—If bread collapses during baking, chances are you have let your bread rise too long in the second rising time.

—To obtain a crunchy crust, brush loaves with cold water 10 minutes after baking begins, then again every 10 minutes.

—For a sheen on the bread, brush the bread with egg white mixed with 1 teaspoon (5 ml) water before baking. For a shiny crust, brush with an egg yolk mixed with 1 teaspoon (5 ml) water.

STEP 2 *Mix with the doughmaker for 3 minutes at speed recommended in your instruction book. After 3 minutes, add the minimum amount of flour as stated in the recipe.*

STEP 3 *Knead dough for 3 more minutes. Stop machine. Feel the dough with your hand. If it is sticky, add enough of the remaining 1/2 cup (125 ml) flour so that it is not sticky. The dough will pull away from the sides of the bowl when enough flour has been added. Do not add too much flour or the bread will have a coarse texture and will be heavy. Do not knead for more than 7 minutes. To adapt your own recipes to the "Kitchen Center" appliance, follow the procedure of steps 1, 2 and 3. Use active dry yeast and no more than 7 cups (1.75 liters) flour.*

STEP 5 *Check to see if the dough has doubled by pressing two fingers 1/2" (1.25 cm) into the dough. If the imprint remains, the dough has doubled. Punch dough down with a fist, removing air bubbles. Gather dough into a ball.*

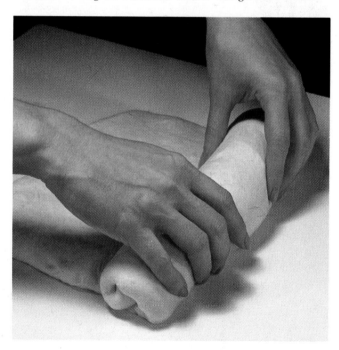

STEP 4 *Gather dough into a ball and place in a greased bowl. Turn the dough over so that all sides of dough have a layer of fat on the outside. Cover and allow to rise in a warm place, around 85°F (30°C) until it has doubled (unless directed otherwise in recipe).*

STEP 6 *To shape a loaf for a 9×5×3-inch (23×13×8 cm) loaf pan, follow these steps. Roll half of the dough (if a 2 loaf recipe) into a 14×7-inch (36×18 cm) rectangle with a rolling pin. Roll up tightly jelly roll style from smaller side. Pinch seam and ends with fingers to seal. Put seam side down in greased pan. Bake until golden brown. Loaf is done if it sounds hollow when tapped.*

"KITCHEN CENTER" FOOD GRINDER

The Oster "Kitchen Center" food grinder can be used to grind meat, nuts, bread, vegetables, cheese, fruits and much more. When used in conjunction with the sausage maker accessory, it can even make your favorite sausages. Doing it yourself with the Oster "Kitchen Center" food grinder helps stretch the family food budget.

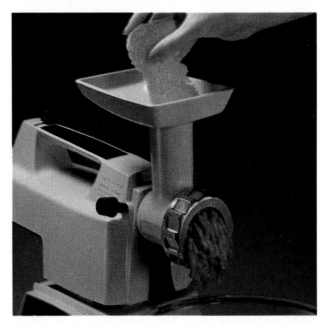

CLEANING GRINDER *To clean food from food grinder, grind half a piece of bread. When bread is visible on grinding disc, turn unit off. Doing this pushes remaining food from grinder, eliminating waste, and making clean up easier.*

GRINDING MEAT *Assemble food grinder as directed in your Instruction Book and attach to your "Kitchen Center" appliance. Turn the unit on, then off and retighten the retaining ring. Always use the food grinder at the highest speed. Cut pieces of food to be ground just smaller than the size of the hopper opening. When grinding meat, fat may be trimmed if desired, but some should be left for best flavor. For grinding meat, use the Fine Disc for a butcher shop grind, the Coarse Disc for a chunkier grind. Alternate the ingredients through the grinder when two or more ingredients to be ground are to be mixed together. For example, alternate meat cubes, bread, and onion for meatloaf to reduce the amount of mixing necessary.*

GRINDING NUTS AND FRUITS *Grind nuts, candied and dried fruit with the Coarse Disc to achieve a chopped texture. Use the Fine Disc for a very fine ground texture. Do not use the food pusher when grinding nuts, the nuts will self feed. When grinding almonds, turn the machine on and drop almonds in the hopper one by one.*

GRINDING CHEESE *Grind cheese for cheese balls using either the Coarse or Fine Disc. Grind cooked liver for liver pate and cooked ham, beef, pork and egg for sandwich spreads. The "Kitchen Center" food grinder helps you stretch the family food budget by using "leftovers" for sandwiches.*

CANNING *The food grinder is a great canning companion. Grind cabbage, pepper, onions, tomatoes, cucumbers and cranberries with the Coarse Disc for relishes. Grind strawberries, rhubarb, apples, peaches, pears, and oranges for jams, also with the Coarse Disc.*

SAUSAGE MAKER *The sausage maker kit (an optional accessory) extends the use of your "Kitchen Center" appliance. The kit includes a small, medium and large stuffing tube along with an extra-coarse grinding disc for all your favorite sausages — from Kielbasa to breakfast links to Italian Sausage to Bratwurst. Homemade sausages have a controlled amount of fat and no additives and preservatives.*

"KITCHEN CENTER" MIXER

The Oster "Kitchen Center" mixer satisfies all your mixing needs from the heaviest cookie doughs to whipping fluffy egg whites. The 1 1/2 quart (1.5 liter) and 4 quart (4 liter) mixing bowls aid you in mixing a very small amount to large amounts of ingredients. The mixing guide on the Mixer Arm should be used as a guide for selecting speeds when using your own recipes. Adjust speeds as needed. To adjust the speed on your "Kitchen Center" model for recipes in this book, refer to "Know Your Mixer" on page 29.

SMALL MIXING BOWL *The small mixer bowl should be used when mixing small quantities, such as frostings, dips and spreads, and when whipping cream and 4 or less egg whites. Be sure to use the turntable in the proper position.*

LARGE MIXER BOWL *Beat egg whites for Angel Food Cake in the large mixer bowl. Be sure to position turntable in proper position. Use the mixer for recipes in this book along with all your family standard favorites.*

ADJUSTING SPEEDS *When mixing flour or powdered sugar with other ingredients, mix at LOW speed until moistened, then increase to recommended speed for the recipe. The wide range of speeds allows you to fold in ingredients at the lowest speed and whip quickly at the highest speed.*

"KITCHEN CENTER" ACCESSORIES

Blend 'N Store containers, both 8-ounce (250 ml) and 30-ounce (1 liter), are handy for blending foods, then storing for future use. The 30-ounce (1 liter) containers are great for mixing orange juice, pancake batters, and salad dressings. The 8-ounce (125 ml) "Mini-Blend" containers are perfect for blending and storing baby food, coffee beans, sauces and more!

BABY FOOD *Prepare baby's food at home in the blender from family meals. Season the family meals after a portion has been taken out for baby. Use "Mini-Blend" containers to purée cooked fruits, vegetables and meats, mixed with a small amount of liquid, then store until needed. Preparing your own baby food not only lets you control your baby's diet — it saves money, too!*

30-OUNCE (1 LITER) CONTAINERS
To use Blend 'N Store containers, put ingredients to be processed into Blend 'N Store container. Put processing blades on jar, tighten retaining ring. Turn container over and place on motor base. Use 30-ounce (1 liter) Blend 'N Store containers for mixing frozen juice concentrates, reconstituting powdered milk, mixing salad dressing and pancake batter. Cover and store in refrigerator.

BABY FOOD *Both strained and junior baby food can be prepared in "Mini-Blend" containers. Blend strained food for small infants longer than food for older babies. To test for smoothness, rub a small amount of baby food between your index finger and thumb.*

GRINDING COFFEE *Grind whole coffee beans in "Mini-Blend" containers. Put 1/2 cup (125 ml) beans into blender container, process 10 cycles at GRIND for percolator coffeemakers or 15 cycles at GRIND for drip coffeemakers. Cover and store any unused coffee right in the jar. You can't beat that fresh ground flavor.*

"KITCHEN CENTER" ACCESSORIES

Oster has a full line of accessories to extend the use of your "Kitchen Center" appliance. Besides Blend 'N Store containers, cutting discs, and the sausage stuffing kit, an ice crusher, "Power Purée 'N Ricer" accessory, citrus juicer, juice extractor and can opener are available. Why clutter your counter with many small appliances when you can add a small attachment to your "Kitchen Center" appliance?

ICE CRUSHER *Use the ice crusher attachment to crush ice for use in cocktails, for relish trays, shrimp cocktails, keeping butter cold, and for making ice cream — wherever crushed ice is needed. Continuous feed feature allows you to crush large quantities of ice.*

JUICE EXTRACTOR *The juice extractor accessory separates the pulp from juice of fresh fruits and vegetables such as apples, carrots and tomatoes. A variety of fresh juice combinations can be processed for healthful vitamin packed refreshments.*

PASTA ACCESSORY *Use the Pasta Accessory to make fresh, homemade pasta. Mix the dough with the mixer and then feed the dough into the grinder hopper. The five discs included allow you to make thin and thick Spaghetti, Lasagna, Rigatoni, and Fettucini. A measuring/storage container, pasta auger, cleaning tool, and recipe book are also included.*

"POWER PUREE 'N RICER" ACCESSORY *The "Power Purée 'N Ricer" accessory processes soft fruits and vegetables to a smooth consistency. It takes all the work out of preparing applesauce, tomato sauce, whatever you want to purée by separating peels and seeds from the purée. Use the "Power Purée 'N Ricer" accessory for preparing foods for canning and freezing, ricing potatoes, preparing baby foods and gourmet fruit and vegetable preparations.*

CITRUS JUICER *The citrus juice accessory juices limes, lemons and oranges as well as grapefruits in seconds. Seeds and pulp remain in the citrus juicer, while the fruit juice flows into your glass. To obtain the most juice from fruit, bring fruit to room temperature before juicing.*

Proper Speed Selection

The "Instruction Book" that was packed with your unit is your basic guide to proper speed selection and operation of your model Oster "Kitchen Center" appliance. Keep it handy to answer any questions.

"Kitchen Center" Blender

Your Oster "Kitchen Center" blender speeds are found on the front of the base and range from STIR to LIQUEFY. Each speed can be run continuously or cycled with the pulse button. The names on the base should be used as a guide for speed selection. Adjust speed as necessary. Recipes in this book state the speed and kind of operation — continuous operation or cycle.

"Kitchen Center" Mixer

For your convenience we have included a handy "Kitchen Center" mixer Speed Selection Guide, "Know Your Mixer." Recipes in this book use speeds from LOW, MEDIUM-LOW, MEDIUM, MEDIUM-HIGH, and HIGH instead of specific mixer speed names such as CREAMING or WHIPPING.

To use the chart
1. Note the suggested mixer speed in the recipe.
2. Locate that speed on the left hand column of the chart and follow along on the chart to your "Kitchen Center" model.

The words on the Mixer Arm are to be used as a guide in mixing your own recipes. After locating the appropriate word describing your mixing action on the Mixer Arm, set the motor speed to the corresponding number on the Speed Selection Dial. Adjust speed as necessary.

KNOW YOUR MIXER

RECIPE DIRECTION	10 SPEED	12 SPEED	16 SPEED
LOW	1 FOLDING 2 STIRRING	1 FOLDING 2 STIRRING	1 FOLDING 2 STIRRING 3 MOISTEN
MEDIUM LOW	3 MIXING 4 CREAMING	3 MIXING 4 CREAMING 5 CAKES	4 MIXING 5 CREAMING 6 CAKES
MEDIUM	5 CAKES 6 MASHING	6 MASHING 7 HEAVY MIXING	7 BLENDING 8 MASHING 9 HEAVY MIXING 10 SAUCES
MEDIUM HIGH	7 BEATING 8 FROSTINGS-CANDIES	8 BEATING 9 FROSTINGS 10 CANDIES	11 BEATING 12 FROSTINGS 13 CANDIES
HIGH	9 WHIPPING 10 KNEADING-GRINDING	11 WHIPPING 12 KNEADING-GRINDING	14 WHIP CREAM 15 WHIPPING 16 KNEADING-GRINDING

"Kitchen Center" "FoodCrafter" Slicer/Shredder/Salad Maker

Speed selection for use with the "Kitchen Center" Salad Maker depends on the food you are processing. Hard foods are processed at a higher speed than delicate or soft foods. Consult your "Instruction Book" for correct speeds for your unit. Remember, these speeds are only guides. When there are variations in food textures because of different degrees of ripeness, speeds may need to be adjusted.

"Kitchen Center" Food Grinder

The powerful "Kitchen Center" food grinder should always be used with the highest speed setting.

"Kitchen Center" Doughmaker

Consult your "Kitchen Center" "Instruction Book" for the correct speed to knead bread in your "Kitchen Center" model.

"Kitchen Center" Accessories

Each Oster "Kitchen Center" accessory has its own "Instruction Book." Be sure to consult the book for the correct speed to operate each of our many versatile accessory appliances.

Your Wake-Up Call

One of the best new-fashioned dimensions of the Oster "Kitchen Center" appliance is that it can restore old-fashioned breakfast pleasures: the fragrance of freshly squeezed orange juice, the economy of pancakes made "from scratch," the incomparable taste of homemade sweet rolls. You can use the appliance to grind coffee beans and make juicy sausage patties, to knead coffeecakes and create puffy omelets. There are no better ways to say "Good morning!"

For brunchtime entertaining, the "Kitchen Center" unit turns easily to the menu elegance of Broccoli or Mushroom Quiche and Spinach Cheese Tarts baked in crêpe shells. When everyone is in a hurry, the "Osterizer" Blender whips up the batter for Apple Cinnamon Pancakes or the whole-meal nutrition of Breakfast in a Glass. When there's time for a leisurely gathering, the family can linger over Ham Patties and Egg Casserole, with Apple Squares or Swedish Coffeecake. And don't overlook recipes in other chapters for many more breakfast selections.

Egg Casserole

Try this egg dish with coffeecake at your next special breakfast or brunch.

- 9 **eggs**
- 1/2 **cup (125 ml) milk**
- 1 **small onion, quartered**
- 1/2 **green pepper, seeded and halved**
- 1 **can (10 3/4 ounces or 305 g) condensed cream of mushroom soup**
- 6 **slices pasteurized process American cheese**

Assemble Blender. Put eggs, milk, onion, and green pepper into blender container. Cover and process at CHOP until onion and green pepper are finely chopped. Pour into a large skillet and cook over medium-high heat, stirring constantly to scramble eggs. Spoon cooked eggs into a greased 2-quart (2 liter) casserole. Pour soup over eggs and top with cheese slices. Cover with lid or foil and set in refrigerator at least 8 hours or overnight. Bake covered at 350°F (180°C) for 35 to 40 minutes.

6 servings

Ham Patties

Here's a great use for that leftover ham.

    1/2 pound (227 g) cooked ham, cut in
           1-inch (2.5 cm) pieces
    1/2 small onion
    1/8 teaspoon (0.5 ml) pepper
      2 eggs, beaten
      1 tablespoon (15) dried
           parsley flakes

Assemble Food Grinder with Fine Disc. Grind ham and onion (about 2 cups or 500 ml) into small mixing bowl. Add pepper, eggs, and parsley; mix well. Drop by teaspoonfuls onto greased hot griddle over medium heat; cook, lightly browning both sides.

12 small patties

Hollandaise Sauce

Pour over poached eggs and Canadian-style bacon for classic Eggs Benedict, or serve on cooked green vegetables.

      4 egg yolks
    1/4 teaspoon (1 ml) dry mustard
      1 tablespoon (15 ml) lemon juice
           Dash hot pepper sauce
    1/2 cup (125 ml) melted butter

Assemble Blender. Put all ingredients except butter into blender container. Cover and process at MIX. Remove feeder cap and pour butter in a slow, steady stream until mixture is completely emulsified. Keep warm over hot (not boiling) water.

3/4 cup (200 ml)

Swedish Coffeecake

Serve this butter-rich coffeecake warm.

    1/2 cup (125 ml) melted butter
  1 1/2 cups (375 ml) sugar
  1 1/2 cups (375 ml) all-purpose flour
      2 teaspoons (10 ml) baking powder
    1/2 teaspoon (2 ml) salt
      1 egg
    2/3 cup (150 ml) milk
      1 teaspoon (5 ml) ground cinnamon

Preheat oven to 375°F (190°C). Assemble Mixer. In small mixer bowl, mix 2 tablespoons (30 ml) melted butter, 1 cup (250 ml) sugar, flour, baking powder, salt, egg, and milk at LOW until flour is moistened then at MEDIUM-HIGH until smooth. Pour into a greased 8-inch (20 cm) round baking pan. Drizzle with remaining melted butter. Mix remaining sugar and cinnamon; sprinkle over top. Bake for 35 to 40 minutes, or until toothpick inserted near center comes out clean. Cool completely, then slice into eight wedges.

8 servings

Orange-Banana Breakfast

This is breakfast for the banana lovers in your family.

      1 ripe medium banana, peeled and sliced
    1/4 cup (50 ml) skim milk
      1 tablespoon (15 ml) frozen orange
           juice concentrate, thawed
      1 egg

Assemble Blender. Put all ingredients into blender container. Cover and process at LIQUEFY until smooth.

1 serving, 230 calories

Sour Cream Coffee Cake

The addition of sour cream in a coffeecake is a classic old-world idea to ensure a tender, moist texture.

1 1/2 cups (375 ml) sugar
  2 teaspoons (10 ml) ground cinnamon
  1 cup (250 ml) pecans
 1/2 cup (125 ml) solid shortening
  2 eggs
  1 teaspoon (5 ml) vanilla extract
  2 cups (500 ml) all-purpose flour
1 1/2 teaspoons (7 ml) baking powder
 1/2 teaspoon (2 ml) baking soda
 1/2 teaspoon (2 ml) salt
  1 carton (8 ounces or 227 g) dairy
    sour cream

Preheat oven to 350°F (180°C). Assemble Blender. Put 1/2 cup (125 ml) sugar, cinnamon, and pecans into blender container. Cover and process 5 cycles at GRIND or until nuts are finely chopped; set aside. Assemble Mixer. In large mixer bowl, cream remaining sugar, shortening, eggs, and vanilla extract at MEDIUM-LOW. Combine remaining dry in-gredients. Add alternately with sour cream until smooth. Spread half of batter in a greased 8-cup (2 liter) springform pan with tube insert. Sprinkle with half the sugar mixture. Bake 45 to 50 minutes, or until toothpick inserted near center comes out clean. Cool slightly before removing from pan. Serve immediately, or cool, wrap, and store in freezer for up to 2 months.

10 to 12 servings

Broccoli Quiche

This quiche can be served as a main dish for brunch.

  1 package (10 ounces or 284 g)
    frozen chopped broccoli, thawed
    and drained
  1 unbaked 9-inch (23 cm) pie shell
    (see Standard Pastry, page 154)
  1 cup (250 ml) light cream
  2 eggs
 1/4 teaspoon (1 ml) ground nutmeg
  1 small onion, quartered
  1 cup (250 ml) sharp Cheddar
    Cheese cubes (1 inch or 2.5 cm)
 2/3 cup (150 ml) Swiss cheese cubes
    (1 inch or 2.5 cm)

Preheat oven to 350°F (180°C). Pat broccoli into pie shell and spread evenly. Assemble Blender. Put remaining in-gredients into blender container. Cover and process at CHOP until onion and cheese are finely chopped. Bake 45 minutes, or until knife inserted in center comes out clean. Cut into wedges to serve.

About 8 servings

Cheese Pancakes with Strawberries

Cottage cheese pancakes topped with sour cream and strawberries are a great special breakfast.

- 3/4 cup (200 ml) milk
- 1/2 cup (125 ml) small curd creamed cottage cheese
- 2 teaspoons (10 ml) sugar
- 1/2 teaspoon (2 ml) baking powder
- 2 eggs
- 3/4 cup (200 ml) all-purpose flour
- 1/2 teaspoon (2 ml) ground cinnamon
- Dairy sour cream
- Sweetened sliced strawberries

Assemble Blender. Put milk and cottage cheese into blender container. Cover and process at PUREE until smooth. Add sugar, baking powder, eggs, flour, and cinnamon. Cover and process at BLEND until smooth. Bake on hot buttered griddle over medium heat pouring about 2 tablespoons (30 ml) batter for each pancake and turning when bubbles appear on upper surface and begin to break. When browned on both sides, serve topped with sour cream and strawberries.

14 to 20 pancakes

Apple Cinnamon Pancakes

Apple and cinnamon are mixed into the batter for these tasty pancakes.

- 1 1/2 cups (375 ml) milk
- 2 eggs
- 1/3 cup (75 ml) solid shortening
- 1 1/2 cups (375 ml) all-purpose flour
- 2 1/2 teaspoons (12 ml) baking powder
- 1/2 teaspoon (2 ml) salt
- 1 teaspoon (5 ml) ground cinnamon
- 2 medium apples, quartered, pared, and cored (1 cup or 250 ml apple quarters)

Assemble Blender. Put all ingredients into blender container. Cover and process at MIX until apples are finely chopped. For each pancake, pour a small amount of batter on a greased hot griddle and bake over medium heat, turning when bubbles appear on upper surface and begin to break. Serve hot with butter and syrup.

18 pancakes

Strawberry Yogurt Frost

A cool, tangy refresher for kids and adults.

- 1 carton (10 ounces or 284 g) frozen sliced strawberries
- 1/3 cup (75 ml) instant nonfat dry milk
- 1 cup (250 ml) plain yogurt
- 3/4 cup (200 ml) water
- 1 teaspoon (4 ml) vanilla

Assemble Blender. Cut frozen block of strawberries in half. Put milk, yogurt, water, strawberries, and vanilla into blender container. Cover and process at LIQUEFY until smooth.

3 1/2 cups (875 ml)

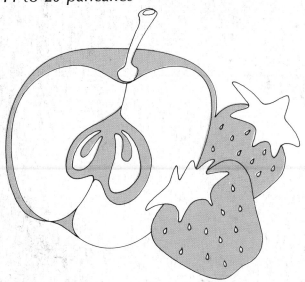

Apple Cinnamon Pancakes, Cheese Pancakes with Strawberries

Danish Kringle

This flaky coffeecake can be filled with cheese, fruit, nut, or poppy seed filling.

1 1/2 **cups (375 ml) water**
1/2 **cup (125 ml) butter or margarine**
3 **cups (750 ml) all-purpose flour**
1 **package (1/4 ounce or 7 g) active dry yeast**
1/3 **cup (75 ml) instant nonfat dry milk**
1 1/2 **tablespoons (23 ml) sugar**
1/2 **teaspoon (2 ml) salt**
1 **egg yolk**
1/2 **cup (125 ml) all-purpose flour Filling (opposite)**
1 **egg white**

Heat water and butter to 120°F (48°C). Assemble Doughmaker. In large mixer bowl, combine 3 cups (750 ml) flour, yeast, dry milk, sugar, salt, egg yolk, and warmed mixture. Mix with doughmaker at recommended speed for 3 minutes, or until smooth. (It may be necessary to scrape sides of bowl with rubber spatula and rotate bowl slightly by hand.) The dough will be very soft. Cover bowl with plastic wrap and chill for at least 2 hours or no more than 48 hours. Prepare desired filling before shaping dough. Grease 2 cookie sheets. Using pastry cloth, generously rub about one half of remaining flour into cloth and rolling pin cover. Punch down and divide dough into two portions. Put one portion on pastry cloth and return the other to refrigerator. Coat dough with flour then roll with rolling pin into 18×6-inch (45×15 cm) rectangle. Beat egg white until foamy. Spread center 3 inches (7.5 cm) with one half of beaten egg white, then with 1/3 to 1/2 cup (75 to 125 ml) filling. Fold over one side of dough then the other with 1 1/2-inch (3.8 cm) overlap to cover filling. Pinch dough to seal. Put Kringle on cookie sheet, shaping either in an oval or horseshoe. Prepare second Kringle. Cover and let rise in a warm place for 30 to 45 minutes, or until a dent remains when finger is pressed gently in side of dough. Dough should no longer feel cold. Bake in preheated 400°F (200°C) oven for 20 to 30 minutes, or until golden brown. Spread with Confectioners Sugar Glaze (page 37) while hot. Cool on wire racks. Cut into wedges to serve.

2 Kringles or about 24 servings

Almond Filling

1 **cup (250 ml) almond paste, cut in teaspoon-size pieces**
1 **cup (250 ml) confectioners sugar**
1 **egg**

Assemble Mixer. In small mixer bowl, mix almond paste, sugar, and egg at MEDIUM-LOW until blended.

1 cup (250 ml)

Cheese Filling

1 1/3 **cups (325 ml) dry cottage cheese**
2 **egg yolks**
1 **tablespoon (15 ml) melted butter**
1/3 **cup (75 ml) light corn syrup**

Assemble Blender. Put ingredients into blender container. Cover and process at BLEND until smooth. Pour into saucepan. Cook over medium heat, stirring occasionally, until thickened; do not boil. Cool.

1 2/3 cups (400 ml)

Date Nut Filling

    1/2 cup (125 ml) pecans or walnuts
    1/2 pound (227 g) pitted dates
  1 1/4 cups (300 ml) water
    1/2 cup (125 ml) sugar

Assemble Blender. Put pecans into blender container. Cover and process 4 cycles at WHIP to finely chop nuts. Empty container and set nuts aside. Put dates and water into blender container. Cover and process at BLEND until dates are chopped into small pieces. Pour into saucepan and bring to a boil. Add sugar and simmer for 15 minutes. Stir in chopped nuts and cool.

2 cups (500 ml)

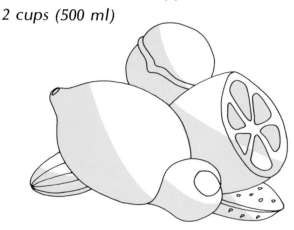

Pecan Filling

    1 cup (250 ml) pecans
  1/4 cup (50 ml) butter or margarine,
         at room temperature
  1/2 cup (125 ml) firmly packed
         brown sugar

Assemble Blender. Put pecans into blender container. Cover and process 2 cycles at WHIP to chop nuts; set aside. Assemble Mixer. In small mixer bowl, cream butter and sugar at MEDIUM-LOW until fluffy. Stir in chopped pecans.

1 1/2 cups (375 ml)

Poppy Seed Filling

    1 cup (250 ml) poppy seed
  3/4 cup (200 ml) milk
  1/3 cup (75 ml) honey
    1 tablespoon (15 ml) grated
         lemon peel
    2 tablespoons (30 ml) lemon juice
    2 tablespoons (30 ml) butter
    1 egg yolk

Assemble Blender. Put poppy seed into blender container. Cover and process at GRIND until seeds are crushed. Empty into saucepan and stir in remaining ingredients. Cook over medium heat until thick, stirring as necessary. Cool.

1 2/3 cups (400 ml)

Raisin Filling

    2 tablespoons (30 ml) butter or
         margarine, at room temperature
  1/2 cup (125 ml) firmly packed
         brown sugar
    1 cup (250 ml) plump seedless
         raisins
    2 teaspoons (10 ml) almond extract

Assemble Mixer. Cream butter and sugar at MEDIUM-LOW. Add raisins and almond extract and mix well.

1 1/3 cups (325 ml)

Confectioners Sugar Glaze

    1 cup (250 ml) confectioners sugar
    1 tablespoon (15 ml) light cream
         or half-and-half
  1/4 teaspoon (1 ml) vanilla extract

Assemble Mixer. In small mixer bowl, mix all ingredients at LOW until spreading consistency.

1/2 cup (125 ml)

Filled Sweet Rolls

See the other fillings on pages 36 and 37 that can be used in these sweet rolls.

Basic Quick Sweet Dough (page 60)

Custard Filling

1 tablespoon (15 ml) all-purpose flour
2 tablespoons (30 ml) sugar
2 egg yolks
1 cup (250 ml) light cream
    or half-and-half
2 teaspoons (10 ml) vanilla extract

Prepare Basic Quick Sweet Dough, then Custard Filling. For filling, combine flour and sugar in small saucepan. Stir in egg yolks and cream. Cook over low heat, strirring occasionally, until thick and smooth. Add vanilla extract, stir, and cool. When dough is doubled, punch down, divide into two portions, and roll each to about 1/2-inch (1.3 cm) thickness. Cut with floured large cookie cutter. Put dough rounds onto cookie sheet. Make indentations in centers and crimp edges. Spoon about 1 tablespoon (15 ml) filling into center of each. (Or cut into squares and spoon filling onto centers. Bring two opposite corners of each to center and pinch to seal. Put onto cookie sheets.) Cover and let rise until doubled. Bake in preheated 375°F (190°C) oven for 15 to 20 minutes, or until lightly browned.

About 2 dozen

Orange and Yogurt

A meal in a glass — great for those rushed days.

2 large oranges
1 egg
1/4 cup (50 ml) honey
1 container (8 ounces or 227 g) plain
    low fat yogurt

Assemble Citrus Juicer. Juice oranges into glass (about 1 cup or 250 ml.) Assemble Blender. Put juice and remaining ingredients into blender container. Cover and process at LIQUEFY until well mixed. Serve immediately.

2 servings, 280 calories for each serving

Apricot-Strawberry Breakfast Cocktail

This healthful fruited milk drink will give your day a bright beginning.

1 can (8 3/4 ounces or 248 g)
    apricot halves with syrup
3/4 cup (200 ml) fresh strawberries
3/4 cup (200 ml) milk
4 to 6 ice cubes

Assemble Blender. Put apricots, syrup, strawberries, and milk into blender container. Cover and process at LIQUEFY. With motor running, remove feeder cap and add ice cubes one at a time until mixture is cold and smooth.

4 servings

Breakfast Kuchen

These two large coffeecakes will serve a crowd, or serve one now and freeze the other.

Basic Quick Sweet Dough (page 60)
1 cup (250 ml) walnuts
1 cup (250 ml) butter or margarine, at room temperature
1 cup (250 ml) sugar

Prepare Basic Quick Sweet Dough; let dough rise in greased bowl as directed. Meanwhile, assemble Salad Maker with Shredder Disc and large mixer bowl. Process nuts; set aside. Assemble Mixer. In small mixer bowl, cream butter and sugar at MEDIUM-LOW, adding nuts near the end. Set aside. Punch down, cut dough in half, and roll each half into a rectangle about 13 1/2×8 1/2 inches (34×21 cm). Put dough into a greased 15 1/2×10 1/2×1-inch (39×27×3 cm) jelly roll pan. Spread with half of butternut mixture. Repeat with second half of dough. Let rise in warm place until doubled (about 45 minutes). Bake in preheated 350°F (180°C) oven for 20 to 25 minutes, or until top is golden brown. Cut into squares to serve.

48 servings

Apple Squares

This apple-filled coffeecake can be made ahead and frozen for that special family breakfast.

1 1/2 cups (375 ml) all-purpose flour
1 tablespoon (15 ml) sugar
1 teaspoon (5 ml) baking powder
1/2 cup (125 ml) butter, at room temperature
1 egg yolk
2 tablespoons (30 ml) milk
5 large tart apples, pared and cored
2/3 cup (150 ml) sugar
2 tablespoons (30 ml) all-purpose flour
1/2 teaspoon (2 ml) ground cinnamon
2 tablespoons (30 ml) melted butter

Preheat oven to 375°F (190°C). Assemble Mixer. In small mixer bowl, combine first six ingredients at MEDIUM-LOW until mixed. Pat into an 8×8×2-inch (20×20×5 cm) baking pan. Assemble Salad Maker with Thin Slicer Disc and large bowl. Process apples. Spread apples evenly over butter crust. Stir remaining ingredients together and spoon over apples. Bake in preheated oven for 45 to 50 minutes, or until golden brown. Cool 30 minutes before cutting into squares.

9 servings

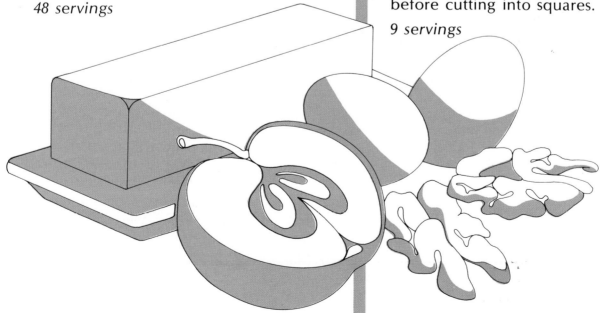

Breakfast in a Glass

Have a nourishing, low calorie start to the day!

> 2 **eggs**
> 1 **cup (250 ml) skim milk**
> 1 **cup (250 ml) fresh fruit pieces**
> 3 **tablespoons (45 ml) honey**
> 2 **tablespoons (30 ml) wheat germ**
> 4 **ice cubes**

Assemble Blender. Put all ingredients except ice cubes into blender container. Cover and process at LIQUEFY. With motor running, remove feeder cap and add ice cubes, one at a time. Continue to processs until smooth.

2 servings, 285 calories for each serving

Mushroom Quiche

Mushrooms add a certain something to Swiss cheese custard pie.

> 4 **ounces (113 g) fresh mushrooms**
> 4 **eggs**
> 1 1/2 **cups (375 ml) light cream or**
>   **half-and-half**
> 1 **tablespoon (15 ml) all-purpose flour**
> 1/2 **teaspoon (2 ml) salt**
> 1/4 **teaspoon (1 ml) white pepper**
> 1/4 **teaspoon (1 ml) ground nutmeg**
> 1 1/2 **cups (375 ml) Swiss cheese cubes**
>   **(1 inch or 2.5 cm)**
> 1/2 **medium onion, quartered**
> 5 **slices bacon, crisp fried and**
>   **crumbled (1/3 cup or 75 ml)**
> 1 **unbaked 9-inch (23 cm) pie shell**
>   **(see Standard Pastry, page 154)**

Assemble Salad Maker with Thick Slicer Disc. Process mushrooms (2 cups or 500 ml); set aside. Assemble Blender. Put eggs, cream, flour, salt, pepper, and nutmeg into blender container. Cover and process at MIX until well blended. Stop Blender and add Swiss cheese and onion. Cover and process 5 cycles at GRIND to chop cheese and onion. Put bacon and mushrooms in bottom of pie shell. Pour egg mixture into pie shell. Bake in preheated 375°F (190°C) oven for 40 to 45 minutes, or until a knife inserted in center comes out clean.

8 servings

Puffy Chive Omelet

This well-seasoned omelet is baked in the oven.

> 8 **eggs, at room temperature**
> 3 **tablespoons (45 ml) all-purpose**
>   **flour**
> 3 **tablespoons (45 ml) milk**
> 2 **teaspoons (10 ml) chopped chives,**
>   **fresh or frozen**
> 1/2 **teaspoon (2 ml) salt**
> 1/2 **teaspoon (2 ml) onion salt**
> 1 **teaspoon (5 ml) dry mustard**
> 1/4 **teaspoon (1 ml) Worcestershire sauce**
>   **Dash white pepper**

Separate eggs; put yolks into small mixer bowl and whites into large mixer bowl. Assemble Mixer. Beat egg yolks at MEDIUM until creamy. Beat in flour, milk, chives, salt, onion salt, mustard, Worcestershire, and pepper. Wash beaters and dry. Beat egg whites until stiff but not dry at HIGH. Carefully pour yolk mixture over whites; mix at LOW just until blended. Spoon into well-buttered shallow 2-quart (2 liter) casserole or soufflé dish. Bake in preheated 350°F (180°C) oven for 30 to 35 minutes, or until golden brown. Serve immediately.

6 servings

Puffy Chive Omelet, Breakfast in a Glass, Mushroom Quiche

Spinach Cheese Tarts

Crêpes instead of pastry form the shells for these spinach tarts.

    8 crêpes (see Basic Crêpe Recipe,
        page 59)
    4 ounces (113 g) Swiss cheese, chilled
   10 small fresh mushrooms
    1 tablespoon (15 ml) all-purpose flour
    3 eggs
  1/2 cup (125 ml) Blender Mayonnaise
        (page 97)
  1/2 package (10-ounce or 284 g size)
        frozen chopped spinach, thawed and
        thoroughly drained
  1/2 teaspoon (2 ml) salt
    4 slices bacon, crisp fried
        and crumbled

Fit crêpes into greased muffin cups, forming fluted tart shells. Preheat oven to 350°F (180°C). Assemble Salad Maker with Shredder Disc and large bowl. Process cheese. Change disc to French Fry Cutter. Process mushrooms. Add flour, toss to coat, and set aside. Assemble Mixer. In small mixer bowl, beat eggs at LOW until blended. Add mayonnaise, drain spinach, salt, cheese, and mushrooms; beat at LOW until mixed. Spoon into prepared crêpe tart shells. Sprinkle with bacon. Bake for 30 minutes.

8 servings

Parmesan Butter

Put an end to plain toast with this spread.

    2 cubes (1-inch or 2.5 cm)
        Parmesan cheese
    1 cup (250 ml) whipping cream
    1 sprig parsley, stem removed

Assemble Blender. Cover blender container and set at GRIND. With motor on, drop cheese through feeder cap. Continue to process until cheese is finely grated. Add cream and parsley. Cover and process at CHOP until butter forms (about 10 minutes). (If necessary, STOP BLENDER, use rubber spatula to keep mixture around processing blades. Cover and continue to process.) Pour into strainer to drain off liquid. Put into small bowl and press with spatula to remove as much liquid as possible. Add salt, if desired.

1 cup (250 ml)

Frosty Eggnog

A traditional holiday treat that can be enjoyed all year 'round.

    4 eggs
  1/4 cup (50 ml) water
    1 cup (250 ml) instant nonfat
        dry milk
    3 tablespoons (45 ml) sugar
  1/2 teaspoon (2 ml) rum extract
  1/2 teaspoon (2 ml) vanilla
        Dash nutmeg
   12 ice cubes

Assemble Blender. Put eggs, water, milk, sugar, rum extract, vanilla, nutmeg, and 6 ice cubes into blender container. Cover and process at LIQUEFY until smooth. With motor on, remove feeder cap and gradually add remaining ice cubes. Continue to process until smooth. Pour into cups and sprinkle with additional nutmeg.

3 cups

Hey! What's For Lunch?

Diverse ingredients and imaginative combinations hold the key to soup and sandwich satisfactions. Temptation is a juicy burger piled high with all kinds of fixings, a bowl of soup afloat with nuggets of vegetables, or a sandwich layered like a Dagwood dream! With the Oster "Kitchen Center" appliance all your temptations become tasty treats in a matter of minutes.

Use the "Osterizer" Blender and Salad Maker for all vegetable cutting and chopping chores. The Blender and "Power Purée 'N Ricer" accessory yield the silken textures of Creamy Asparagus Soup, Carrot Soup, and no-cook Chilled Chicken Curry Soup as well as the joy of homemade Peanut Butter. The Food Grinder opens a world of hamburger possibilities — all fresher and leaner than purchased ground beef. And the combined talents of the Doughmaker, Food Grinder, and Salad Maker produce the best Deep Dish Jumbo Pizza you've ever tasted!

Cream of Tomato Soup

The thickening for this soup is potato juice extracted from fresh potato put through the Juice Extractor.

     8 **medium tomatoes**
     2 **tablespoons (30 ml) butter**
        or margarine
 1 1/2 **teaspoons (7 ml) sugar**
   1/2 **teaspoon (2 ml) salt**
        Dash onion powder
        Dash celery salt
        Dash pepper
   1/4 **cup (50 ml) potato juice**
     2 **cups (500 ml) milk**

Assemble Juice Extractor. Process tomatoes at recommended speed; you should have 2 cups (500 ml) juice. Put tomato juice, butter, sugar, salt, onion powder, celery salt, and pepper into 2-quart (2 liter) saucepan. Heat over medium heat. Add potato juice to milk. Stir into hot tomato mixture and heat until slightly thickened.

1 quart (1 liter)

Carrot Soup

The vegetable purée thickens this golden soup.

    2 pounds (907 g) carrots
    2 medium onions
    2 small potatoes
    1 bay leaf
    1 quart (1 liter) chicken broth
    2 cups (500 ml) milk
  1/4 teaspoon (1 ml) salt
       Dash pepper

Cook carrots, onions, potatoes, and bay leaf covered in 3-quart (3 liter) saucepan with chicken broth until vegetables are tender. Cool slightly. Remove bay leaf. Assemble Puréer. Process carrots, onions, and potatoes with liquid at HIGH into 3-quart (3 liter) saucepan. Add remaining ingredients, mix well, heat thoroughly.

8 servings

Cucumber Soup

This light soup is good either hot or chilled.

    3 large cucumbers, pared, halved
         and seeded
    1 can (10 3/4 ounces or 305 g)
         condensed chicken broth
    1 cup (250 ml) light cream
    1 stalk celery, cut in 1-inch
         (2.5 cm) pieces
    1 tablespoon (15 ml) chopped chives
    1 sprig parsley, stems removed
    1 teaspoon (5 ml) dill weed
    2 tablespoons (30 ml) butter, at
         room temperature
    2 tablespoons (30 ml) all-purpose flour

Assemble Salad Maker with French Fry Cutter Disc and large bowl. Process cucumbers; set aside. Assemble Blender.

Put remaining ingredients into blender container. Cover and process at CHOP until celery is finely chopped. Put cucumber and chicken broth mixture into medium saucepan over low heat; stir constantly until hot and slightly thickened.

4 to 6 servings

Country Vegetable Soup

When the weather turns windy and cold, a bowl of this hot soup and crisp rye rolls will be warming.

  1 1/2 pounds (681 g) fresh broccoli
      4 carrots, pared
      1 medium zucchini, halved lengthwise
      1 medium onion, halved
      1 green pepper, halved and seeded
      1 clove garlic, minced
    1/2 pound (227 g) cooked ham, cut in
           1-inch (2.5 cm) pieces
      3 cups (750 ml) chicken broth
      3 cups (750 ml) water
      1 teaspoon (5 ml) salt
    1/2 teaspoon (2 ml) pepper
      2 cups (500 ml) uncooked broken
           thin spaghetti

Wash broccoli and break into small pieces, removing woody stems. Assemble Salad Maker with Thick Slicer Disc and large bowl. Process broccoli, carrots, and zucchini. Change disc to French Fry Cutter Disc and process onion and green pepper. Put into 6-quart (6 liter) Dutch oven. Add remaining ingredients except spaghetti and bring to a boil over high heat. Reduce heat and simmer covered 30 minutes, or until vegetables are tender. Add spaghetti and cook covered over medium heat 10 minutes.

8 to 10 servings

Chilled Chicken Curry Soup

After mixing in the blender, this soup is ready to serve.

- 1 **cup (250 ml) milk**
- 1 **can (10 3/4 ounces or 305 g) condensed cream of chicken soup**
- 1 **tablespoon (15 ml) shredded coconut**
- 1 **teaspoon (5 ml) curry powder**
- 1/2 **teaspoon (2 ml) salt**
- 1/2 **teaspoon (2 ml) ground mace**
- 1/4 **apple, pared and cored**
- 1 **cup (250 ml) ice cubes**

Assemble Blender. Put all ingredients except ice into blender container. Cover and process at PUREE until smooth. Stop blender and add ice. Cover and process at LIQUEFY until ice is liquefied.

4 servings

Note: If a thinner soup is preferred, add more milk.

Chinese Vegetable Soup

The Orient will seem as close as your kitchen when you serve this tangy soup with its pea pods and water chestnuts.

- 1 **2 1/2-pound (1 kg) frying chicken**
- 1 **can (8 ounces or 227 g) water chestnuts, drained**
- 1 **small green pepper, quartered and seeded**
- 1 **small onion, halved**
- 6 **large fresh mushrooms**
- 1 **package (6 ounces or 170 g) frozen Chinese pea pods**
- 1/3 **cup (75 ml) soy sauce**

Put chicken into 5-quart (5 liter) Dutch oven, cover with water, and simmer covered for 1 hour, or until chicken is tender. Remove chicken and set aside to cool. Measure chicken broth; add water if necessary to make 5 cups (1.3 liters). Return to Dutch oven. Assemble Salad Maker with Thick Slicer Disc and large bowl. Process water chestnuts, green pepper, onion, and mushrooms. Add to Dutch oven. Bring to a boil and simmer covered until vegetables are just tender (about 15 minutes). Meanwhile, skin and bone chicken; cut chicken into pieces. Add chicken and pea pods to soup. Simmer covered for 5 minutes. Just before serving, stir in soy sauce.

6 to 8 servings

Potato Halibut Soup

This fish-vegetable soup is topped with seasoned uncooked red onion.

- 1 **pound (454 g) potatoes, pared**
- 1 **large onion, quartered**
- 1 1/2 **quarts (1.5 liters) chicken broth**
- 1 **teaspoon (5 ml) dill weed**
- 2 **pounds (907 g) halibut fillets, cut in 1-inch (2.5 cm) pieces**
- 1 **medium mild red onion**
  Salt and white pepper
  Dill weed for garnish

Assemble Salad Maker with French Fry Cutter Disc. Process potatoes and onion into large saucepan. Add broth and dill weed. Bring to a boil and simmer covered until vegetables are almost tender (about 10 minutes). Add fish pieces and simmer covered until fish flakes when tested with a fork (about 3 minutes). Meanwhile, with French Fry Cutter Disc, process red onion into small bowl. Ladle soup into serving bowls; top with spoonful of uncooked onion. Season with salt, pepper, and dill weed.

6 servings

Creamy Asparagus Soup

Serve this creamy-smooth soup as a dinner first course or luncheon main dish.

3 1/2 cups (875 ml) chicken broth
   3 tablespoons (45 ml) all-purpose flour
   3 tablespoons (45 ml) butter, at
      room temperature
   2 egg yolks
1/2 teaspoon (2 ml) salt
1/4 teaspoon (1 ml) pepper
   1 package (10 ounces or 284 g) frozen
      cut asparagus, thawed
   1 cup (250 ml) light cream

Assemble Blender. Put 1 1/2 cups (375 ml) chicken broth and remaining ingredients except cream into blender container. Cover and process at GRATE until smooth. Pour into a 3-quart (3 liter) saucepan and add remaining broth. Heat slowly over medium heat, stirring constantly; add cream just before serving.

6 to 8 servings

Creamed Carrot and Potato Soup

The carrots give a golden color to this nourishing soup.

   4 medium potatoes, pared
      and quartered
   3 large carrots, pared and quartered
   1 medium onion, quartered
   1 stalk celery, cut in 4 pieces
   2 teaspoons (10 ml) salt
   1 tablespoon (15 ml) butter or
      margarine, at room temperature
   1 tablespoon (15 ml) all-purpose flour
   2 cups (500 ml) milk
   1 teaspoon (5 ml) seasoned salt
1/4 teaspoon (1 ml) white pepper
    Minced parsley

Put vegetables into large saucepan, cover with water, and add 1 teaspoon (5 ml) salt. Bring to a boil and cook covered until very tender (20 to 25 minutes). Assemble Blender. Put butter, flour, 1 teaspoon (5 ml) salt, and milk into blender container. Cover and process at WHIP until well blended. Pour into saucepan and cook over low heat, stirring constantly until slightly thickened. Put cooled vegetables and liquid into blender container. Cover and process at LIQUEFY until puréed. Empty blender container into saucepan with sauce. Stir and heat; do not boil. Stir in seasoned salt and pepper. Garnish with parsley.

2 quarts (2 liters)

Blender Gazpacho

Serve this soup very cold in chilled soup bowls.

1/2 cup (125 ml) chicken broth, chilled
   1 clove garlic, quartered
1/2 small onion, diced
1/2 green pepper, seeded and cut in
      1-inch (2.5 cm) pieces
   1 can (16 ounces or 454 g) tomatoes,
      cut in pieces
   1 small cucumber, pared, seeded,
      and sliced
   1 teaspoon (5 ml) salt
1/2 teaspoon (2 ml) basil leaves
1/4 teaspoon (1 ml) freshly ground pepper
   3 tablespoons (45 ml) wine vinegar
   2 tablespoons (30 ml) olive oil

Assemble Blender. Put all ingredients into blender container. Cover and process 2 cycles at BLEND to coarsely chop vegetables. Chill before serving. If desired, thin soup with chilled chicken broth.

6 servings

Winter Vegetable Beef Soup

Beef and seven vegetables make a hearty soup.

        1   tablespoon (15 ml) vegetable oil
1 1/2 to 2   pounds (681 to 907 g) beef
              chuck with bone
        1   quart (1 liter) warm water
        2   teaspoons (10 ml) salt
        1   bay leaf
        3   medium potatoes, pared and quartered
        2   large onions, quartered
        2   medium carrots, pared
        1   green pepper, quartered and seeded
     1/2   small head cabbage, cut in wedges
        1   package (10 ounces or 284 g) frozen
              green peas (optional)
        1   can (28 ounces or 793 g) tomatoes,
              undrained
1 1/2   teaspoons (7 ml) savory
     1/4   teaspoon (1 ml) pepper

Heat oil in 5-quart (5 liter) Dutch oven. Over medium heat; add meat and brown on both sides. Turn heat to low; add warm water, salt, and bay leaf. Simmer covered until meat is fork tender (about 1 1/2 hours). Remove meat and trim, discarding bone; shred meat and return to broth. Assemble Salad Maker with French Fry Cutter Disc and large bowl. Process all vegetables except peas and tomatoes. Cut tomatoes into pieces. Add all vegetables to broth including peas and tomatoes with liquid. Simmer covered until potatoes and carrots are tender (about 1 hour). Stir in savory and pepper.

6 to 8 servings

Beef Vegetable Soup

Serve crisp rolls or crackers with this hearty meal-in-a-bowl soup.

        2   cans (10 1/2 ounces or 298 g each)
              condensed beef broth
        2   soup cans water
1 1/2   pounds (681 g) beef chuck, cut in
              1-inch (2.5 cm) pieces
     1/2   cup (125 ml) ketchup
     1/4   teaspoon (1 ml) pepper
        1   medium onion, halved
        2   stalks celery, cut in 4-inch
              (10 cm) pieces
        6   carrots, pared
        1   package (9 ounces or 255 g) frozen
              cut green beans
     1/2   cup (125 ml) barley

Put broth, water, beef, ketchup and pepper into a 5-quart (5 liter) Dutch oven. Assemble Salad Maker with Thick Slicer Disc and large bowl. Process onion, celery, and carrots. Add processed vegetables, beans, and barley to soup; stir well. Bring to a boil and simmer covered 2 hours, or until meat is very tender.

6 to 8 servings

Peanut Butter

Use wherever peanut butter is called for in recipes.

1 1/2 cups (375 ml) salted cocktail peanuts

Assemble Blender. Put peanuts into blender container. Cover and process at BLEND to the desired consistency. (If necessary, STOP BLENDER, use rubber spatula to keep mixture around processing blades. Cover and continue to process.)

3/4 cup (200 ml)

Gallic Cabbage Soup

A typical French creamy vegetable soup.

- 2 **medium onions, halved**
- 2 **medium potatoes, pared and halved**
- 2 **medium carrots, pared**
- 1 **small head cabbage (1 1/4 pounds or 567 g), cut in wedges**
- 2 **tablespoons (30 ml) butter**
- 1 **quart (1 liter) chicken broth**
- 1 1/2 **teaspoons (7 ml) salt**
- 1/2 **teaspoon (2 ml) ground thyme**
- 1/4 **teaspoon (1 ml) white pepper**
- 1 **cup (250 ml) light cream or**

Assemble Salad Maker with French Fry Cutter Disc and large bowl. Process onion; set aside. Process potato, carrot, and cabbage. In skillet, heat butter and sauté onion until limp. Bring chicken broth to a boil in large saucepan. Add sautéed onion, processed vegetables, salt, thyme, and pepper. Simmer covered until vegetables are tender but not mushy (about 35 minutes). Stir in cream; heat but do not boil. Serve hot.

6 servings

Ham 'n' Egg Sandwiches

Try also as a quick appetizer using party rye bread.

- 1 **pound (454 g) cooked ham, cut in 1-inch (2.5 cm) pieces**
- 2 **hard-cooked eggs, halved**
- 1 **medium onion, quartered**
- 1 **package (8 ounces or 227 g) cream cheese, at room temperature**
- 1 **cup (250 ml) Blender Mayonnaise (page 97)**
- 1 **teaspoon (5 ml) dry mustard**
  Rye bread slices

Assemble Food Grinder with Fine Disc. Grind ham, eggs, and onion into large mixer bowl. Assemble Mixer. Add cream cheese, mayonnaise, and dry mustard to ham mixture and mix at LOW then at MEDIUM-LOW until well mixed. Generously spread on slices of rye bread and broil for 5 minutes, or until bread is toasted and ham mixture is hot. Serve immediately.

8 to 10 servings

Beef Barbecue Sandwiches

These sandwiches would be a good choice for the lunch crowd.

- 2 **pounds (907 g) boneless beef chuck, cut in 1-inch (2.5 cm) pieces**
- 2 **medium onions, quartered**
- 1 **cup (250 ml) ketchup**
- 1/2 **cup (125 ml) water**
- 2 **tablespoons (30 ml) sugar**
- 2 **tablespoons (30 ml) prepared mustard**
- 2 **tablespoons (30 ml) vinegar**
- 2 **teaspoons (10 ml) salt**
- 1/4 **teaspoon (1 ml) pepper**
  Hamburger buns

Assemble Food Grinder with Fine Disc. Grind meat and onion into small bowl. Put meat into heated large skillet and cook until browned, stirring as necessary. Drain off excess fat. Assemble Blender. Put ketchup, water, sugar, mustard, vinegar, salt, and pepper into blender container. Cover and process at BLEND until smooth. Pour over meat and bring to a boil. Reduce heat and simmer 10 minutes to blend flavors. Serve hot in hamburger buns.

12 to 14 servings

Deep Dish Jumbo Pizza

This is a hearty meal that is fun to prepare for a party.

- **1 pound (454 g) boneless pork, cut in 1-inch (2.5 cm) pieces**
- **1/2 pound (227 g) boneless beef chuck, cut in 1-inch (2.5 cm) pieces**
- **1 cup (250 ml) milk**
- **2 tablespoons (30 ml) solid shortening**
- **2 cups (500 ml) all-purpose flour**
- **1 package (1/4 ounce or 7 g) active dry yeast**
- **1 tablespoon (15 ml) sugar**
- **1 teaspoon (5 ml) salt**
- **1 egg**
- **1 can (15 ounces or 425 g) tomato sauce**
- **1 tablespoon (15 ml) dried Italian seasoning**
- **1/2 green pepper, seeded**
- **1 medium onion, halved**
- **10 pitted large ripe olives**
- **10 large mushrooms, cleaned**
- **1 pound (454 g) Mozzarella cheese, chilled**

Assemble Food Grinder with Fine Disc. Grind meat into large bowl. Put meat into heated large skillet; cook until browned, stirring as necessary. Drain off excess fat; set aside. Heat milk and shortening to 120°F (48°C); set aside. Assemble Doughmaker. In small mixer bowl, put flour, yeast, sugar, salt, warmed mixture, and egg. Mix with doughmaker at recommended speed for 5 minutes. (This is a yeast batter and will be thin.) Grease a 15 1/2 × 10 1/2 × 1-inch (39 × 27 × 3 cm) jelly roll pan. With rubber spatula, spread batter evenly over bottom and up sides of pan. Spread tomato sauce over dough and sprinkle with Italian seasoning. Assemble Salad Maker with Thin Slicer Disc and large bowl. Process green pepper, onion,

olives, and mushrooms. Arrange evenly over tomato sauce. Change disc to Shredder Disc. Process cheese (about 4 cups or 1 liter). Evenly spoon cooked meat over vegetables. Sprinkle cheese over meat. Bake in preheated 425°F (220°C) oven for 20 to 25 minutes. Let stand for 5 minutes before cutting into squares.

4 to 6 servings

Variation: If desired, substitute 1 1/2 pounds (681 g) bulk Italian sausage for ground pork and beef. Cook and drain as directed.

Sweet and Sour Burgers

A sauerkraut and cranberry sauce mixture tops these onion burgers.

- **1 envelope (1.35 ounces or 38 g) onion soup mix**
- **1/2 cup (125 ml) water**
- **1 egg, beaten**
- **1 1/2 pounds (681 g) boneless beef chuck, cut in 1-inch (2.5 cm) pieces**
- **1 cup (250 ml) sauerkraut, drained**
- **3/4 cup (200 ml) whole cranberry sauce**
- **1/4 cup (50 ml) chili sauce**
- **3 tablespoons (45 ml) brown sugar**
- **6 onion rolls**

Combine onion soup mix, 1/4 cup (50 ml) water, and egg in large bowl. Assemble Food Grinder with Fine Disc. Grind beef into the bowl; mix thoroughly. Shape into 6 patties. Put sauerkraut, cranberry sauce, chili sauce, brown sugar, and remaining water into small saucepan; mix well. Simmer 20 minutes, stirring occasionally. Split and toast onion rolls. Broil or grill meat patties to degree of doneness desired. Put patties on buns and top with sauerkraut mixture..

6 servings

Pocket Salad Sandwiches (page 52), Sweet and Sour Burgers, Deep Dish Jumbo Pizza

Pocket Salad Sandwiches

Prepare Pita Bread and have ready to fill. Or use packaged pita bread for a quick substitute.

- 1/3 **cup (75 ml) olive oil**
- 1/3 **cup (75 ml) tarragon vinegar**
- 3/4 **teaspoon (3 ml) salt**
- 1/4 **teaspoon (1 ml) pepper**
- 2 **green onions, cut in 1-inch (2.5 cm) pieces**
- 2 **sprigs parsley, stems removed**
- 1 **cup (250 ml) cut fresh green beans, cooked and drained**
- 1 **can (6 1/2 ounces or 184 g) chunky tuna, drained**
- 1/2 **cup (125 ml) raisins**
- 6 **hard-cooked eggs, halved**
- 6 **pita breads (see page 65)**
- 12 **lettuce leaves**
- 2 **medium tomatoes, peeled and coarsely chopped**
- 1 **jar (6 ounces or 170 g) marinated artichoke hearts, drained and quartered**

Assemble Blender. Put oil, vinegar, salt, and pepper into blender container. Cover and process at BEAT until blended. Add green onion, parsley, and green beans. Cover and process at BEAT until chopped. Empty into refrigerator container. Stir in tuna and raisins. Cover; chill for several hours. Shortly before serving, assemble Blender. Put 2 eggs into blender container. Cover and process 2 cycles at STIR, or until chopped. Empty chopped egg into a bowl. Repeat with remaining eggs, chopping 2 at a time. Cut or break each pita bread in half crosswise. Open pocket. Tuck a lettuce leaf in bottom of each pocket. Top with tuna mixture, chopped tomato, artichoke heart pieces, and chopped egg.

6 servings

Cheese and Ripe Olive Sandwiches

Serve these hot open-face sandwiches with soup or as an appetizer.

- 1 **cup (250 ml) Cheddar cheese cubes (1 inch or 2.5 cm)**
- 1/2 **small onion**
- 1/3 **cup (75 ml) pitted ripe olives**
- 1/3 **cup (75 ml) Blender Mayonnaise (page 97)**
- 1/8 **teaspoon (0.5 ml) curry powder Rye bread slices (large or party rye size)**

Assemble Food Grinder with Coarse Disc. Grind cheese, onion, and olives into bowl. Mix mayonnaise and curry powder; stir into cheese mixture. Spread on bread and broil 4 inches (10 cm) from heat until tops are lightly browned (2 to 3 minutes).

6 large or 18 party rye size sandwiches

Hamburgers

Basic burgers with freshly ground beef go creative in many ways.

> 2 pounds (970 g) boneless beef chuck, shoulder, or round, cut in 1-inch (2.5 cm) pieces
> 1 1/2 teaspoons (7 ml) salt
> 1/2 teaspoon (2 ml) pepper

Assemble Food Grinder with Fine Disc. Grind meat into large bowl. Lightly mix in salt and pepper. Shape into eight patties. Broil on both sides until brown, or cook in a little butter in a skillet over medium heat. Do not overcook.

8 servings

Filled Hamburgers: Follow recipe for Hamburgers. Divide each pattie in half and pat into thin patties. Put a thin slice of onion or cheese or both on one pattie, top with second pattie, and press together at edges. Cook as directed.

Onion Hamburgers: Follow recipe for Hamburgers, grinding 1 or 2 medium onions, quartered, with meat. Mix lightly but well before shaping into patties.

Hawaiian Hamburgers: Mix 1 can (8 3/4 ounces or 248 g) crushed pineapple, drained, and 1/2 cup (125 ml) flaked coconut. Set aside. Follow recipe for Hamburgers, mixing 1 tablespoon (15 ml) soy sauce and 1/2 teaspoon (2 ml) ground ginger with meat. Shape into patties. Cook as directed. Top each pattie with 1 tablespoon (15 ml) pineapple-coconut mixture.

Italian Hamburgers: Follow recipe for Hamburgers, grinding 1 small onion with meat. Mix in 1 teaspoon (5 ml) oregano leaves. Shape into patties, broil. Top each patty with slice of Mozzarella cheese, and broil to melt cheese. Top with hot canned pizza sauce.

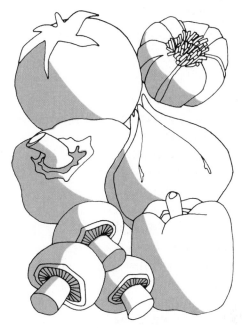

Cucumber Sandwiches

A cool, crisp sandwich filling that can double as a cracker spread for a cocktail party.

> 1 medium cucumber, pared, halved, and seeded
> 1 small onion, quartered
> 1 package (8 ounces or 227 g) cream cheese, at room temperature
> 1/2 cup (125 ml) Blender Mayonnaise (page 97)
> 1/2 teaspoon (2 ml) salt
> 1/4 teaspoon (1 ml) pepper
> Whole wheat bread slices
> Lettuce leaves

Assemble Salad Maker with Shredder Disc and large bowl. Process cucumber. Change disc to Thin Slicer Disc and process onion. Assemble Mixer. Mix cream cheese, mayonnaise, salt, and pepper with cucumber and onion at MEDIUM-LOW until well mixed. Chill. Spread on bread, allowing 1/4 to 1/3 cup (50 to 75 ml) filling for each sandwich. Top filling with crisp lettuce leaves.

6 to 8 servings

Greek Style Pocket Bread

The unusual and pleasing blend of flavors makes this a favorite hearty sandwich special.

- 1 **pound (454 g) boneless sirloin steak, partially frozen and cut in paper-thin strips**
- 1 **small onion, halved**
- 1/2 **medium green pepper, seeded and halved**
- 6 **large fresh mushrooms**
- 1/4 **cup (50 ml) red wine vinegar**
- 2 **tablespoons (30 ml) sesame seed oil or olive oil**
- 1 **clove garlic**
- 1/2 **teaspoon (2 ml) salt**
- 1/2 **teaspoon (2 ml) oregano leaves**
- 1/4 **teaspoon (1 ml) pepper**
- 6 **pita breads (see page 65)**
  Topping (optional):
  Cucumber, coarsely chopped
  Tomato, coarsely chopped
  Alfalfa sprouts
  Dairy sour cream

Put steak strips into large bowl. Assemble Salad Maker with French Fry Cutter Disc. Process onion, green pepper, and mushrooms into bowl with steak. Put vinegar, oil, and seasonings into "Mini-Blend" container and process at CHOP until garlic is finely minced. Pour over steak and vegetables; cover. Refrigerate for 1 hour. Pour steak and vegetables into a large skillet and cook over medium-high heat. Cut or break pita bread in half crosswise. With slotted spoon, fill pocket with filling. If desired, top filling with cucumber, tomato, alfalfa sprouts, and/or dairy sour cream.

6 servings

Arabian Style Pocket Bread

Lamb flavored with mint and cinnamon is a change-of-pace filling for sandwiches.

- 1 **pound (454 g) boneless lamb shoulder, cut in paper-thin slices**
- 1/4 **cup (50 ml) peanut or other vegetable oil**
- 1/4 **cup (50 ml) olive oil**
- 3 **green onions, cut in 1-inch (2.5 cm) pieces**
- 1/2 **teaspoon (2 ml) dried mint**
- 1/2 **teaspoon (2 ml) ground cinnamon**
- 3 **sprigs parsley, stems removed**
- 2 **tablespoons (30 ml) butter, at room temperature**
- 2 **tablespoons (30 ml) all-purpose flour**
- 1 **cup (250 ml) milk**
- 1 **clove garlic**
- 1/2 **teaspoon (2 ml) dill weed**
- 4 **pita breads (see page 65)**

Put lamb into small bowl. Assemble Blender. Put oils, onion, mint, cinnamon, and parsley into "Mini-Blend" container and process at CHOP until onion is finely chopped. Pour over meat and cover. Refrigerate for 1 hour. Drain off and discard marinade. Brown meat in medium skillet until meat is cooked. Remove from heat. Assemble Blender. Put remaining ingredients except pita bread into blender container. Cover and process at CHOP until garlic is minced. Pour into skillet with meat and heat slowly, stirring constantly until sauce is thickened. Stir to coat meat. Cut or break pita breads in half crosswise and fill with meat mixture.

4 servings

Bake, Batter & Bowl

Simple techniques for yeast loaves, batter breads, rolls, and refrigerated doughs translate into an international sampler of fabulous baking: from Old-Fashioned White Bread and Peasant Rye Bread to Soft Dough Pretzels, Glazed Doughnuts, and a half dozen kinds of Crêpes.

All of the yeast loaf recipes use the quick-mix method; so you don't have to proof the yeast before you mix the dough. Even if you have never baked bread before, the Doughmaker ensures effortless kneading and even texture. Safeguard your results by adding extra flour only as needed; the amount needed to produce a smooth dough will depend on the humidity in the air and, to a lesser degree, on the brand of flour.

The fastest loaf formulas are moist batter breads like Apricot Orange Nut Bread, Pineapple Zucchini Bread, and Cranberry Cheddar Bread — especially when you have the "Osterizer" Blender and Salad Maker to chop and shred the nuts, fruits, and vegetables. The easily kneaded dough for Bran or Potato Refrigerator Rolls will keep for several days — ready to rise and pop in the oven whenever you're ready for fresh-baked bread.

Honey Corn Bread

The perfect complement for fried chicken!

1	cup (250 ml) all-purpose flour
2	cups (500 ml) yellow cornmeal
1 1/4	cups (300 ml) milk
1/2	cup (125 ml) honey
1/3	cup (75 ml) vegetable oil
2	eggs
1	tablespoon (15 ml) baking powder
1/8	teaspoon (0.5 ml) salt

Preheat oven to 400°F (200°C). Assemble Mixer. In large bowl, mix all ingredients at MEDIUM-LOW until well blended. Pour into a greased 9-inch (23 cm) square baking pan. Bake 30 minutes, or until toothpick inserted near center comes out clean.

9 servings

Golden Sesame Braid

The braids whether baked on cookie sheets or in loaf pans are impressive.

1 1/2 cups (375 ml) milk
   2 tablespoons (30 ml) butter
     or margarine
   3 cups (750 ml) all-purpose flour
   2 packages (1/4 ounce or 7 g each)
     active dry yeast
1/4 cup (50 ml) sugar
   1 teaspoon (5 ml) salt
   3 eggs
   2 tablespoons (30 ml) Oriental
     sesame oil or vegetable oil
   3 to 3 1/2 cups (750 to 875 ml)
     all-purpose flour
   1 egg yolk
   1 tablespoon (15 ml) water
   2 tablespoons (30 ml) sesame seed

Heat milk and butter to 120°F (48°C). Assemble Doughmaker. In large mixer bowl, combine 3 cups (750 ml) flour, yeast, sugar, salt, eggs, oil, and warmed mixture. Mix with doughmaker at recommended speed for 3 minutes. (It may be necessary to scrape sides of bowl with rubber spatula and rotate bowl slightly by hand.) Add 3 cups (750 ml) flour and continue kneading for 3 minutes. If dough is sticky, knead in enough of remaining 1/2 cup (125 ml) flour to form a moderately stiff dough. Put dough into greased bowl, turning once to grease the top. Cover and let rise in warm place until doubled (about 30 minutes). Punch down and divide into six equal portions. Shape each portion into a smooth ball, cover, and let rest for 10 minutes. Roll each into a 12-inch (30 cm) strip. Braid three strips to form a loaf and put onto greased cookie sheet. (If desired, tuck ends of braid under and fit into a greased 9 1/4×5 1/4×2 3/4-inch or 23×13×8 cm loaf pan.) Cover and let rise in warm place until doubled (about 45 minutes). Beat egg yolk and water with fork until well mixed. Brush braids with egg mixture and sprinkle each with one half of sesame seed. Bake in preheated 350°F (180°C) oven for 25 to 30 minutes, or until bread sounds hollow when tapped. Remove from cookie sheet and cool on rack.

2 loaves

Spicy Wheat Bread

For a breakfast treat, try spreading bread slices lightly with butter and broiling until hot.

   1 large orange
   2 tablespoons (30 ml) grated
     orange peel
2 1/2 cups (625 ml) whole wheat flour
   1 tablespoon (15 ml) baking powder
1/2 teaspoon (2 ml) baking soda
1/2 cup (125 ml) milk
   1 cup (250 ml) firmly packed
     brown sugar
   1 teaspoon (5 ml) ground allspice
   1 teaspoon (5 ml) ground cinnamon
1/2 teaspoon (2 ml) ground nutmeg
   4 eggs
   1 cup (250 ml) buttermilk
2/3 cup (150 ml) vegetable oil

Preheat oven to 350°F (180°C). Assemble Citrus Juicer. Juice orange (about 1/2 cup or 125 ml) into glass measure. Grate peel of orange (about 2 tablespoons or 30 ml) into large mixer bowl. Assemble Mixer. Add orange juice and remaining ingredients to bowl and mix at LOW until dry ingredients are moistened then at MEDIUM until well mixed. Pour into a greased 9 1/2×5 1/4×2 3/4-inch (23×13×8 cm) loaf pan. Bake 1 hour and 10 minutes, or until toothpick inserted near center comes out clean. Cool thoroughly before removing from pan.

1 loaf

Peasant Rye Bread

This caraway rye bread is shaped in round loaves.

- 1 tablespoon (15 ml) butter
  or margarine
- 1 cup (250 ml) milk
- 1 cup (250 ml) water
- 1 cup (250 ml) all-purpose flour
- 2 1/2 cups (625 ml) rye flour
- 2 packages (1/4 ounce or 7 g each)
  active dry yeast
- 1 tablespoon (15 ml) sugar
- 1 tablespoon (15 ml) caraway seed
- 2 teaspoons (10 ml) salt
- 2 tablespoons (30 ml) honey
- 1 1/2 to 2 cups (375 to 500 ml)
  all-purpose flour
  Yellow cornmeal
- 1 egg yolk
- 1 tablespoon (15 ml) water

Heat butter, milk, and 1 cup (250 ml) water to 120°F (48°C). Assemble Doughmaker. In large mixer bowl, combine 1 cup (250 ml) all-purpose flour, rye flour, yeast, sugar, caraway seed, salt, honey, and warmed mixture. Mix with doughmaker at recommended speed for 3 minutes. (It may be necessary to scrape sides of bowl with rubber spatula and rotate bowl slightly by hand.) Add 1 1/2 cups (375 ml) flour and continue kneading for 3 minutes. If dough is sticky, knead in enough of remaining 1/2 cup (125 ml) flour to form a soft dough. Put dough into greased bowl, turning once to grease top. Cover and let rise in warm place until doubled (about 1 hour). Punch down and divide into two equal portions. Shape each portion into a smooth ball, cover, and let rest for 10 minutes. Sprinkle cornmeal on large cookie sheet or in two 10-inch (25 cm) pie pans. Shape dough into round loaves and put onto cookie sheet. Cover and let rise until doubled (about 45 minutes). Beat egg yolk and 1 tablespoon (15 ml) water with fork until well mixed. Brush lightly over loaf tops. Bake in preheated 350°F (180°C) oven for 30 to 35 minutes. Remove from cookie sheet and cool on racks.

2 loaves

Pineapple Zucchini Bread

The delicate flavor and light texture of this bread is sure to please.

- 1 cup (250 ml) walnuts
- 1 medium zucchini
- 3 eggs
- 1 cup (250 ml) vegetable oil
- 2 cups (500 ml) sugar
- 1 tablespoon (15 ml) vanilla extract
- 1 can (8 ounces or 227 g) crushed
  pineapple, drained
- 3 cups (750 ml) all-purpose flour
- 2 teaspoons (10 ml) baking soda
- 1 teaspoon (5 ml) salt
- 1/2 teaspoon (2 ml) baking powder
- 2 teaspoons (10 ml) ground cinnamon
- 2 teaspoons (10 ml) ground nutmeg

Preheat oven to 350°F (180°C). Assemble Salad Maker with Shredder Disc and large bowl. Process nuts and zucchini. Set aside. Assemble Mixer. In large bowl, beat eggs, oil, sugar, and vanilla extract at MEDIUM-LOW. Add all remaining ingredients. Mix at LOW until dry ingredients are moistened then at MEDIUM-LOW until well combined. Pour into 2 well-greased 8 1/2×4 1/2×2 5/8-inch (22×11×7 cm) loaf pans. Bake 1 hour, or until toothpick inserted near center comes out clean. Cool for 10 minutes before removing from pans.

2 loaves

Basic Crêpe Recipe

A special pancake, really. So easy!

1 1/2 **cups (375 ml) milk**
   2 **tablespoons (30 ml) vegetable oil**
   3 **eggs**
1 1/2 **cups (375 ml) all-purpose flour**
     Dash salt

Assemble Blender. Put all ingredients into blender container in order listed. Cover and process at BLEND until smooth. Use electric crêpe maker following manufacturer's directions or preheat lightly greased sauté pan. Pour in enough batter to cover bottom (scant 1/4 cup or 50 ml); tilt to spread batter thinly and evenly. Flip crêpe when bottom is browned and top is set. Brown second side. To keep for later use, separate crêpes with waxed paper, wrap, and freeze.

20 to 24 crêpes

Parmesan Crêpes: Follow Basic Crêpe Recipe; add 1/2 cup (125 ml) grated Parmesan cheese to blender container. Stir batter frequently while preparing crêpes.

Whole Wheat Crêpes: Follow Basic Crêpe Recipe. Substitute 1 1/4 cups (300 ml) whole wheat flour for all-purpose flour and add 2 tablespoons (30 ml) wheat germ to blender container.

Dessert Crêpes: Follow Basic Crêpe Recipe. Use 1 1/3 cups (325 ml) milk. Add 2 tablespoons (30 ml) orange-flavored liqueur or créme de cacao and 1 tablespoon (15 ml) sugar to blender container.

Chocolate Crêpes: Follow Basic Crêpe Recipe. Add 1/4 cup (50 ml) sugar, 2 tablespoons (30 ml) unsweetened cocoa, and 1 1/2 teaspoons (7 ml) vanilla extract to blender container.

Cornmeal Crêpes: Follow Basic Crêpe Recipe. Add 1/2 cup (125 ml) yellow cornmeal to blender container. Stir batter frequently while preparing crêpes.

Herb Crêpes: Follow Basic Crêpe Recipe. Add 1 teaspoon (5 ml) oregano or thyme or 3 sprigs fresh parsley, stems removed, to blender container.

Lemon Muffins

These muffins are a perfect go-along with your favorite fish dinner.

   1 **lemon**
   1 **cup (250 ml) sugar**
1/2 **cup (125 ml) butter or margarine, at room temperature**
   3 **eggs**
1/4 **teaspoon (1 ml) almond extract**
   2 **cups (500 ml) all-purpose flour**
   1 **teaspoon (5 ml) baking powder**
1/2 **teaspoon (2 ml) salt**

Preheat oven to 375°F (190°C). Assemble Citrus Juicer. Juice lemon into glass measure (about 1/4 cup or 50 ml); set aside. Carefully remove only peel from lemon, put into "Mini-Blend" container, and add 1/2 cup (125 ml) sugar; process 2 or 3 cycles at CHOP, or until peel is finely chopped. Set aside. Assemble Mixer. In large mixer bowl, cream remaining sugar, butter, and eggs at MEDIUM-LOW until smooth. Add lemon-sugar mixture, lemon juice, and remaining ingredients; mix at LOW until flour is moistened. Divide batter equally in 12 paper-lined muffin cups. Bake 15 to 20 minutes. Serve either warm or cool.

12 muffins

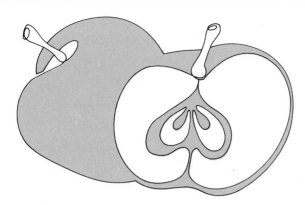

Applesauce Oatmeal Bread

A crisp crust surrounds the wholesomeness of applesauce and oatmeal in this bread.

  2 **eggs**
  1 **cup (250 ml) canned or fresh applesauce (see Note)**
2/3 **cup (150 ml) firmly packed brown sugar**
1 1/2 **cups (375 ml) all-purpose flour**
  1 **teaspoon (5 ml) baking powder**
  1 **teaspoon (5 ml) baking soda**
  1 **teaspoon (5 ml) ground cinnamon**
1/2 **teaspoon (2 ml) ground nutmeg**
1/2 **teaspoon (2 ml) salt**
1/3 **cup (75 ml) vegetable oil**
1 1/2 **cups (375 ml) quick-cooking rolled oats**
3/4 **cup (200 ml) seedless raisins**

Preheat oven to 350°F (180°C). Assemble Mixer. In large mixer bowl, mix all ingredients at LOW until well combined. Pour into a well-greased 8 1/2×4 1/2×2 5/8-inch (22×11×7 cm) loaf pan. Bake in preheated oven for 50 to 60 minutes, or until toothpick inserted near center comes out clean. Cool 10 minutes before removing from pan.

1 loaf

Note: For cooked fresh applesauce, quarter, pare, and core 4 medium cooking apples and put into a saucepan. Add 1/3 cup (75 ml) sugar and 1/3 cup (75 ml)
water; mix well. Bring to a boil and cook covered over medium heat until apples are tender when pierced with fork. Cool. Assemble Blender. Pour contents of saucepan into blender container. Cover and process at PUREE until smooth.

Basic Quick Sweet Dough

Use this yeast dough for coffeecake or rolls.

1 1/4 **cups (300 ml) water**
1/2 **cup (125 ml) butter or margarine**
  3 **cups (750 ml) all-purpose flour**
  2 **packages (1/4 ounce or 7 g each) active dry yeast**
1/2 **cup (125 ml) sugar**
1/3 **cup (75 ml) instant nonfat dry milk**
  1 **teaspoon (5 ml) salt**
  2 **eggs**
2 1/2 **to 3 cups (625 to 750 ml) all-purpose flour**

Heat water and butter to 120°F (48°C). Assemble Doughmaker. In large mixer bowl, combine 3 cups (750 ml) flour, yeast, sugar, dry milk, salt, eggs, and warmed mixture. Mix with Doughmaker at recommended speed for 3 minutes. (It may be necessary to scrape sides of bowl with rubber spatula and rotate bowl slightly by hand.) Add 2 1/2 cups (625 ml) flour and continue kneading for 3 minutes. If dough is sticky, knead in enough of remaining 1/2 cup (125 ml) flour to form a moderately stiff dough. Put dough into greased bowl, turning once to grease top. Cover and let rise in warm place until doubled (about 30 minutes). Punch down and proceed as directed in Breakfast Kuchen or Filled Sweet Rolls on page 39.

Enough dough for two large coffeecakes or two dozen rolls.

Potato Refrigerator Rolls

This refrigerator dough can be shaped into rolls as desired.

- **1 cup (250 ml) mashed potatoes, at room temperature**
- **1 cup (250 ml) milk**
- **1/2 cup (125 ml) water**
- **2/3 cup (150 ml) solid shortening**
- **3 cups (750 ml) all-purpose flour**
- **2 packages (1/4 ounce or 7 g each) active dry yeast**
- **1/2 cup (125 ml) sugar**
- **1 teaspoon (5 ml) salt**
- **2 eggs**
- **3 to 3 1/2 cups (750 to 875 ml) all-purpose flour**

Either boil and mash 2 or 3 medium potatoes or prepare instant mashed potatoes following package directions. Heat milk, water, and shortening to 120°F (48°C). Assemble Doughmaker. In large mixer bowl, combine 3 cups (750 ml) flour, yeast, sugar, salt, mashed potatoes, warmed mixture, and eggs. Mix with doughmaker at recommended speed for 3 minutes. (It may be necessary to scrape sides of bowl with rubber spatula and rotate bowl slightly by hand.) Add 3 cups (750 ml) flour and continue kneading for 3 minutes. If dough is sticky, knead in enough of remaining 1/2 cup (125 ml) flour to form a soft dough. Put dough into greased bowl, turning once to grease top. Cover with plastic wrap and refrigerate until chilled; dough will keep in refrigerator for 2 or 3 days. Punch down and shape dough as desired (see Shaping Rolls, page 68). Cover and let rise at room temperature for about 2 hours. Bake in a preheated 425°F (220°C) oven for about 10 minutes, or until golden brown.

4 dozen rolls

Molasses Cornmeal Bread

You will enjoy the flavor as well as the aroma of molasses in this bread.

- **2 cups (500 ml) water**
- **1/4 cup (50 ml) butter or margarine**
- **2 1/2 cups (625 ml) all-purpose flour**
- **1 cup (250 ml) yellow cornmeal**
- **2 packages (1/4 ounce or 7 g each) active dry yeast**
- **2 teaspoons (10 ml) salt**
- **1/2 cup (125 ml) molasses**
- **3 to 3 1/2 cups (750 to 875 ml) all-purpose flour**

Heat water and butter to 120°F (48°C). Assemble Doughmaker. In large mixer bowl, combine 2 1/2 cups (625 ml) flour, cornmeal, yeast, salt, warmed mixture, and molasses. Mix with doughmaker at recommended speed for 3 minutes. (It may be necessary to scrape sides of bowl with rubber spatula and rotate bowl slightly by hand.) Add 3 cups (750 ml) flour and continue kneading for 3 minutes. If dough is sticky, knead in enough of remaining 1/2 cup (125 ml) flour to form a soft dough. Put dough into greased bowl turning once to grease top. Cover and let rise in warm place until doubled (about 1 hour). Punch down and divide into two equal portions. Shape each portion into a smooth ball, cover, and let rest for 10 minutes. Shape dough into loaves and put into 2 greased 9 1/4×5 1/4×2 3/4-inch (23×13×8 cm) loaf pans. Cover and let rise in warm place until doubled (about 1 hour). Bake in preheated 375°F (190°C) oven for 35 minutes, or until bread sounds hollow when tapped. Remove from pans and cool on racks.

2 loaves

Whole Wheat Banana Bread

This dark, mellow loaf of bread is a pleasing addition to any meal.

    2 ripe bananas, sliced
    1 cup (250 ml) sugar
    1/2 cup (125 ml) melted butter
    2 eggs
    1 cup (250 ml) all-purpose flour
    1/2 teaspoon (2 ml) salt
    1 teaspoon (5 ml) baking soda
    1 cup (250 ml) whole wheat flour
    1/2 cup (125 ml) buttermilk
    1/2 cup (125 ml) raisins

Preheat oven to 325°F (160°C). Assemble Mixer. In large mixer bowl, mix all ingredients except buttermilk and raisins at LOW until dry ingredients are moistened, then at MEDIUM-LOW until well blended. Add buttermilk and raisins; mix at MEDIUM-LOW just until combined. Pour the batter into a well-greased 8 1/2×4 1/2×2 5/8-inch (22×11×7 cm) loaf pan. Bake for 1 hour and 10 minutes, or until toothpick inserted near center comes out clean. Cool completely before removing from pan.

1 loaf

Honey Glaze

    2/3 cup (150 ml) honey
    1/3 cup (75 ml) water
    1/2 cup (125 ml) pecans

Combine honey and water in small saucepan; heat until blended. Chill. Put nuts into "Mini-Blend" container and process 2 cycles at WHIP to chop nuts; set aside. After doughnuts have been fried and drained, dip in chilled honey mixture. Set on rack on waxed paper, sprinkle with nuts, and let dry.

1 cup (250 ml)

Dill Bread

This bread loaf is at its best served warm.

    1 tablespoon (15 ml) instant
        minced onion
    1/4 cup (50 ml) water
    1 cup (250 ml) creamed cottage cheese
    1 tablespoon (15 ml) butter
    1 cup (250 ml) all-purpose flour
    1 package (1/4 ounce or 7 g) active
        dry yeast
    2 tablespoons (30 ml) sugar
    2 teaspoons (10 ml) dill seed
    1 teaspoon (5 ml) baking soda
    1 teaspoon (5 ml) salt
    2 tablespoons (30 ml) wheat germ
    1 egg
1 3/4 to 2 1/4 cups (450 ml to
        550 ml) all-purpose flour
    Melted butter

Heat onion, water, cottage cheese, and butter to 120°F (48°C). Assemble Doughmaker. In large mixer bowl, combine 1 cup (250 ml) flour, yeast, sugar, dill, baking soda, salt, wheat germ, egg, and warmed mixture. Mix with doughmaker at recommended speed for 3 minutes. It may be necessary to scrape sides of bowl with a rubber spatula and to rotate bowl slightly by hand. Add 1 3/4 cups (450 ml) flour and continue kneading 3 more minutes. If dough is sticky, knead in enough of remaining 1/2 cup (125 ml) flour to form a soft dough. Put dough into greased bowl, turning once to grease top. Cover and let rise in warm place until doubled (about 1 hour). Punch down and shape into a loaf. Put into a greased 9 1/4×5 1/4×2 3/4-inch (23×13×8 cm) loaf pan or into two greased 7 1/2×3 3/4×2 1/4-inch (19×10×6 cm) loaf pans. Cover and let rise in warm place until doubled (about 50 minutes). Bake in preheated 350°F (180°C) oven for 30 minutes. Remove from pan and cool on rack. Brush with melted butter. Slice and serve warm.

1 large or 2 small loaves

Whole Wheat Banana Bread, Wheat 'n Raisin Muffins (page 66)

Raised Doughnuts

Three coatings are suggested for these light doughnuts.

1 1/4 **cups (300 ml) milk**
　1/3 **cup (75 ml) butter or margarine**
　　2 **cups (500 ml) all-purpose flour**
　　2 **packages (1/4 ounce or 7 g each)**
　　　　active dry yeast
　3/4 **cup (200 ml) sugar**
　　1 **teaspoon (5 ml) salt**
　　1 **teaspoon (5 ml) ground cinnamon**
　　1 **teaspoon (5 ml) ground mace**
　　　　or nutmeg
　　2 **eggs**
　　3 **to 4 cups (750 to 1000 ml)**
　　　　all-purpose flour
　　　Oil for deep frying
　　　Honey Glaze (page 62),
　　　　confectioners sugar, or
　　　　cinnamon-sugar mixture

Heat milk and butter to 120°F (48°C). Assemble Doughmaker. In large mixer bowl, combine 2 cups (500 ml) flour, yeast, sugar, salt, cinnamon, mace, eggs, and warmed mixture. Mix with doughmaker at recommended speed for 3 minutes. (It may be necessary to scrape sides of bowl with rubber spatula and rotate bowl slightly by hand.) Add 3 cups (750 ml) flour and continue kneading for 3 minutes. If dough is sticky, knead in enough of remaining 1 cup (250 ml) flour to form a moderately stiff dough. Put into greased bowl, turning once to grease top. Cover and let rise in warm place until doubled (about 1 hour). Punch down and turn dough out on lightly floured surface. Cut dough in half. Roll out each half to 1/4-inch (0.6 cm) thickness. Cut with 3 1/2-inch (9.3 cm) or 2 1/2-inch (6.3 cm) doughnut cutter; dip cutter in flour as necessary to prevent sticking. Save holes. Press remainder of trimmings together. Do not reroll dough more than once to avoid toughness. Cover and let rise in warm place until doubled (about 1 hour). Deep fry doughnuts in 370°F (190°C) oil until golden brown, turning once. Drain on paper towels. Spread glaze over warm doughnuts, or shake in confectioners sugar or cinnamon-sugar mixture.

*2 dozen 3 1/2-inch
(9.3 cm) doughnuts*

Bran Rolls

Serve some of these pan rolls fresh from the oven; wrap and freeze the remaining ones, if desired.

1 1/2 **cups (375 ml) water**
　1/2 **cup (125 ml) butter or margarine**
　　1 **cup (250 ml) whole bran cereal**
2 3/4 **cups (700 ml) all-purpose flour**
　　2 **packages (1/4 ounce or 7 g each)**
　　　　active dry yeast
　1/3 **cup (75 ml) instant nonfat**
　　　　dry milk
　1/3 **cup (75 ml) sugar**
　　2 **eggs**
　　2 **teaspoons (10 ml) salt**
2 1/2 **to 3 cups (625 to 750 ml)**
　　　　all-purpose flour

Heat water and butter to 120°F (48°C). Pour over bran cereal. Stir to dissolve. Assemble Doughmaker. In large mixer bowl, combine 2 3/4 cups (700 ml) flour, yeast, dry milk, sugar, eggs, salt, and warmed water mixture. Mix with dough-maker at recommended speed for 3 minutes (it may be necessary to scrape sides of bowl with rubber spatula and rotate bowl slightly by hand.) Add 2 1/2 cups (625 ml) flour and continue kneading for 3 minutes. If dough is sticky, add enough of remaining 1/2 cup (125 ml) flour to form a soft dough. Put dough into greased bowl, turning once to grease top.

Cover and let rise in a warm place until doubled (about 1 hour). Punch down, shape into rolls, about 1 1/2" (3.8 cm) in diameter. Put in 3 greased 8" (20 cm) round pans. Cover and let rise until doubled (about 1 hour). Bake in preheated 375°F (190°C) oven 18-20 minutes.

3 dozen rolls

Bourbon Banana Nut Bread

The flavor of bourbon permeates the baked nut bread during chilling.

3/4 cup (200 ml) walnuts or pecans
1/2 cup (125 ml) butter or margarine, at room temperature
1 cup (250 ml) sugar
2 eggs
2 cups (500 ml) all-purpose flour
1 teaspoon (5 ml) baking powder
1/2 teaspoon (2 ml) baking soda
1/2 teaspoon (2 ml) salt
3 ripe bananas
1 teaspoon (5 ml) vanilla extract
2 tablespoons (30 ml) brown sugar
Bourbon

Preheat oven to 350°F (180°C). Grease a 9 1/4×5 1/4×2 3/4-inch (23×13×8 cm) loaf pan. Assemble Blender. Put nuts into blender container. Cover and process 2 cycles at WHIP to chop nuts; set aside. Assemble Mixer. In large mixer bowl, put all remaining ingredients except 1/4 cup (50 ml) nuts, brown sugar, and bourbon. Mix at LOW until flour is moistened then at MEDIUM until smooth. Pour into prepared pan. Mix remaining nuts and brown sugar; sprinkle over top of loaf. Bake in preheated oven for 1 hour, or until toothpick inserted near center comes out clean. Remove from pan; cool completely. Saturate a 15×9-inch (38×23 cm) double-thick piece of cheesecloth with bourbon and wrap around loaf.

Wrap in foil; refrigerate a few hours or overnight before slicing.

1 loaf

Pita Bread

Bread with pockets that can be filled with any of your favorite hot or cold sandwich fillings.

1 1/2 cups (375 ml) water
2 cups (500 ml) all-purpose flour
1 package (1/4 ounce or 7 g) active dry yeast
1 tablespoon (15 ml) sugar
1 teaspoon (5 ml) salt
2 to 2 1/2 cups (500 to 625 ml) all-purpose flour
Corn meal

Heat water to 120°F (48°C). Assemble Doughmaker. In large mixer bowl, combine 2 cups (500 ml) flour, yeast, sugar, salt, and warmed water. Mix with Doughmaker at recommended speed for 3 minutes. (It may be necessary to scrape sides of bowl with rubber spatula and rotate bowl slightly by hand.) Add 2 cups (500 ml) flour and continue kneading for 3 minutes. If dough is sticky, knead in enough of remaining 1/2 cup (125 ml) flour to form a stiff dough. Put dough into greased bowl, turning once to grease top. Cover and let rise in warm place until doubled (about 45 minutes). Punch down and divide into 6 equal pieces. Roll each piece into 7-inch (18 cm) circles about 1/4-inch (0.6 cm) thick. Put each circle on a cookie sheet and let rise in a warm place until 1/2-inch (1.3 cm) thick (20 to 30 minutes). Sprinkle with corn meal. Bake in a preheated 500°F (260°C) oven for 10 to 15 minutes, or until puffed and lightly browned. Remove from cookie sheet and cool slightly before cutting in half and filling.

6 pita breads

Norwegian Cardamom Bread

For a special holiday bread include both red and green cherries.

1 1/4	cups (300 ml) water
1/2	cup (125 ml) butter or margarine
3	cups (750 ml) all-purpose flour
2	packages (1/4 ounce or 7 g each) active dry yeast
1/2	cup (125 ml) sugar
1/3	cup (75 ml) instant nonfat dry milk
1	teaspoon (5 ml) salt
1	teaspoon (5 ml) freshly ground cardamom
2	eggs
1	cup (250 ml) seedless raisins (golden preferred)
1/2	cup (125 ml) minced citron
1/4	cup (50 ml) chopped candied red cherries, optional
1/4	cup (50 ml) chopped candied green cherries, optional
2 1/4 to 2 3/4	cups (550 to 700 ml) all-purpose flour

Heat water and butter to 120°F (48°C). Assemble Doughmaker. In large mixer bowl, combine 3 cups (750 ml) flour, yeast, sugar, dry milk, salt, cardamom, eggs, and warmed liquid mixture. Mix with doughmaker at recommended speed for 3 minutes. (It may be necessary to scrape sides of bowl with rubber spatula and rotate bowl slightly by hand.) Mix in raisins, citron, and cherries. Add 2 1/4 cups (550 ml) flour and continue kneading for 3 minutes. If dough is sticky, knead in enough of remaining 1/2 cup (125 ml) flour to form a moderately soft dough. The dough will be slightly sticky. Put into greased bowl, turning once to grease top. Cover and let rise in warm place until doubled (1 1/2 to 2 hours). Punch down and divide into 2 equal portions. Shape each portion into a smooth ball, cover, and let rest for 10 minutes. Shape as desired for 2 greased loaf pans 9 1/4×5 1/4×2 3/4-inch (23×13×8 cm) or two 9×1 1/2-inch (23×4 cm) round layer cake pans. Cover and let rise in warm place until doubled (about 1 hour). Bake in preheated 350°F (180°C) oven for 30 to 40 minutes, or until golden brown. Remove bread from pans to cooling rack.

2 loaves bread

Wheat 'n' Raisin Muffins

The nut-like flavor of wheat germ enhances these muffins.

2	eggs
2/3	cup (150 ml) water
1/4	cup (50 ml) butter or margarine, at room temperature
1	teaspoon (5 ml) vanilla extract
1 1/2	cups (375 ml) biscuit mix
2/3	cup (150 ml) toasted wheat germ
1/3	cup (75 ml) sugar
1/4	cup (50 ml) seedless raisins

Preheat oven to 375°F (190°C). Assemble Mixer. In small mixer bowl, put eggs, water, butter, and vanilla extract. Mix at LOW then at MEDIUM-LOW until smooth. In another bowl, stir together biscuit mix, wheat germ, and sugar. Add dry ingredients and raisins to egg mixture. Mix at LOW only until dry ingredients are moistened (do not overmix). Spoon into 12 baking-cup-lined 2 1/2-inch (6.3 cm) muffin cups. Fill cups about two-thirds full. Bake in preheated oven for 20 to 25 minutes, or until lightly browned.

12 muffins

Easy Dinner Rolls

Make a variety of shapes for an interesting basket of rolls.

   1 **cup (250 ml) water**
 2/3 **cup (150 ml) milk**
 1/2 **cup (125 ml) butter or margarine**
   3 **cups (750 ml) all-purpose flour**
   2 **packages (1/4 ounce or 7 g each) active dry yeast**
 1/2 **cup (125 ml) sugar**
 1 1/2 **teaspoons (7 ml) salt**
   3 **eggs**
 2 3/4 **to 3 1/4 cups (700 to 800 ml) all-purpose flour**

Heat water, milk and butter to 120°F (48°C). Assemble Doughmaker with large mixer bowl. Combine 3 cups (750 ml) flour, yeast, sugar, salt, eggs, and warmed mixture. Mix with doughmaker at recommended speed for 3 minutes. (It may be necessary to scrape sides of bowl with rubber spatula and rotate bowl slightly by hand.) Add 2 3/4 cups (700 ml) flour and continue kneading for 3 minutes. If dough is sticky, knead in enough of remaining 1/2 cup (125 ml) flour to form a stiff dough. Put dough into greased bowl, turning once to grease top. Cover and let rise in warm place until doubled (about 1 hour). Punch down and shape rolls as desired (see Shaping Rolls, page 68). Put in greased baking pans as directed. Cover and let rise in warm place until doubled. Bake in preheated 350°F (180°C) oven for 15 to 20 minutes.

4 dozen rolls

Shaping Rolls

Divide dough into pieces about 1 1/2 inches (3.8 cm) in diameter. Shape each into a smooth ball by placing thumb on the bottom of dough, keep pulling dough around thumb until top of roll is smooth. Put, smooth side up, in greased muffin pans or greased 8- or 9-inch (20 or 23 cm) round baking pans (12 rolls per pan).

Easy Cloverleafs

Divide dough into pieces about 1 1/2 inches (3.8 cm) in diameter. Shape as for pan rolls. Put, smooth side up, in greased muffin pan. Dip scissors in flour. Snip top in half, then in half again, forming four points.

Cloverleafs

Divide dough into 1-inch (2.5 cm) pieces. Shape as for pan rolls. Grease muffin pan. Put 3 balls, smooth side up, side by side in each muffin cup.

Crescent Rolls

Divide dough into 5 equal pieces. Using rolling pin, roll each ball into a 12-inch (30 cm) circle.* Cut each circle in 12 wedges. Beginning at wide end, roll dough toward point. Put, point side down, 2 1/2 inches (6.3 cm) apart on greased cookie sheet. Curve ends slightly, forming half-moon shape.

*If desired, dough may be spread with butter at this point.

Parker House Rolls

Roll out dough to 1/4-inch (0.6 cm) thickness. Flour a 2 1/2-inch (6.3 cm) round cutter. Cut out dough, using even pressure. Make an off-center crease in each roll. Fold larger half over smaller half. Put, small side down, 2 1/2 inches (6.3 cm) apart on greased cookie sheets.

Beehives

Pinch off dough into 1 1/2 inch (3.8 cm) diameter pieces. Roll each piece into a rope about 10 inches (25 cm) long. Starting at one end, coil dough into itself, forming a beehive shape. Put 2 1/2 inches (6.3 cm) apart on greased cookie sheet.

Shaping Easy Cloverleafs

Shaping Beehives

Shaping Cloverleafs

Shaping Knots

Shaping Parker House Rolls

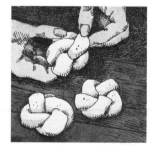
Shaping Fancy Knots

Knots

Divide dough into 1 1/2 inch (3.8 cm) diameter pieces. Roll each piece into a rope about 10 inches (25 cm) long. Tie into a loose knot. Put 2 1/2 inches (6.3 cm) apart on greased cookie sheet.

Fancy Knots

Divide dough into 1 1/2 inch (3.8 cm) diameter pieces. Roll each piece into a rope about 12 inches (30 cm) long. Form into a loose knot, leaving 2 long ends. Bring top end under roll; tuck into center. Bring bottom end up, tucking into center of roll. Put 2 1/2 inches (6.3 cm) apart on greased cookie sheet.

Fennel Breadsticks

These breadsticks go well with salads.

  3/4 cup (200 ml) beer
  1/2 cup (125 ml) water
    2 teaspoons (10 ml) butter or margarine
    2 cups (500 ml) all-purpose flour
    1 package (1/4 ounce or 7 g) active dry yeast
1 1/2 teaspoons (7 ml) salt
    2 teaspoons (10 ml) fennel seed
1 1/2 to 2 cups (375 to 500 ml) all-purpose flour
    1 egg white
    1 tablespoon (15 ml) cold water
     Poppy seed or sesame seed

Heat beer, water, and butter to 120°F (48°C). Assemble Doughmaker. In large mixer bowl, combine 2 cups (500 ml) flour, yeast, salt, fennel seed, and warmed mixture. Mix with doughmaker at recommended speed for 3 minutes. Add 1 1/2 cups (375 ml) flour and continue kneading for 3 minutes. (It may be necessary to scrape sides of bowl with a rubber spatula and to rotate bowl slightly by hand.) If dough is sticky, knead in enough of remaining 1/2 cup (125 ml) flour to form a soft dough. Put dough into greased bowl, turning once to grease top. Cover and let rise in warm place until doubled (about 1 hour). Punch down, turn onto lightly floured board, and divide in half. Roll each piece into an 18-inch (45 cm) roll. Cut into 1-inch (2.5 cm) sections. Roll each piece into a 6-inch (15 cm) rope. Place 1/2-inch (1.3 cm) apart on greased baking sheets. Cover and let rise in warm place for 30 minutes. Beat egg white and water slightly. Brush mixture on sticks and sprinkle with poppy seed. Bake in preheated 400°F (200°C) oven for 20 minutes, or until evenly browned and crispy. Cool on rack.

3 dozen breadsticks

Apricot Orange Nut Bread

A touch of cinnamon enhances the fruit flavor in this colorful loaf.

       2 **large oranges**
   1/2 **cup (125 ml) walnuts**
       6 **2×1-inch (5×2.5 cm) strips orange peel**
       1 **cup (250 ml) dried apricots**
       2 **cups (500 ml) all-purpose flour**
   3/4 **cup (200 ml) sugar**
       1 **tablespoon (15 ml) baking powder**
   1/2 **teaspoon (2 ml) baking soda**
   1/2 **teaspoon (2 ml) salt**
   1/2 **teaspoon (2 ml) ground cinnamon**
       2 **eggs**
       2 **tablespoons (30 ml) vegetable oil**

Preheat oven to 350°F (180°C). Assemble Citrus Juicer. Juice oranges into glass measure (about 1 cup or 250 ml). Assemble Blender. Put nuts into blender container and process 2 cycles at WHIP to chop nuts; set aside. Put orange peel and juice into blender container. Cover and process 4 cycles at PUREE, or until peel is chopped. Add apricots and process 8 cycles at CHOP, or until apricots are chopped. Assemble Mixer. Put all ingredients in large mixer bowl. Mix at LOW until flour is moistened, then at MEDIUM until mixed. Pour into a greased 9 1/4×5 1/4×2 3/4-inch (23×13×8 cm) loaf pan. Bake in preheated oven for 50 to 55 minutes, or until toothpick inserted near center comes out clean. Remove from pan; cool before slicing.

1 loaf

Variation: One cup (250 ml) pitted dried prunes may be substituted for apricots.

Old-Fashioned White Bread

A quick-mix method is used to make this basic white bread.

2 1/4 **cups (550 ml) milk**
       3 **tablespoons (45 ml) butter or margarine**
       3 **cups (750 ml) all-purpose flour**
       2 **packages (1/4 ounce or 7 g each) active dry yeast**
       2 **tablespoons (30 ml) sugar**
       2 **teaspoons (10 ml) salt**
2 3/4 **to 3 1/4 cups (700 to 800 ml) all-purpose flour**

Heat milk and butter to 120°F (48°C). Assemble Doughmaker. In large mixer bowl, combine 3 cups (750 ml) flour, yeast, sugar, salt, and warmed mixture. Mix with doughmaker at recommended speed for 3 minutes. (It may be necessary to scrape sides of bowl with rubber spatula and rotate bowl slightly by hand.) Add 2 3/4 cups (700 ml) flour and continue kneading for 3 minutes. If dough is sticky, knead in enough of remaining 1/2 cup (125 ml) flour to form a stiff dough. Put dough into greased bowl, turning once to grease top. Cover and let rise in warm place until doubled (about 1 hour). Punch down and divide into two equal portions. Shape each portion into a smooth ball, cover, and let rest for 10 minutes. Shape into loaves (see page 23) and put into 2 greased 9 1/4×5 1/4×2 3/4-inch (23×13×8 cm) loaf pans. Cover and let rise in warm place until doubled (45 to 60 minutes). Bake in preheated 375°F (190°C) oven for 10 minutes. Reduce heat to 350°F (180°C) and continue to bake for 30 to 35 minutes. Remove from pans and cool on rack.

2 Loaves

Soft Dough Pretzels

Now you can make your own soft pretzels.

1 1/2 cups (375 ml) water
    2 cups (500 ml) all-purpose flour
    1 package (1/4 ounce or 7 g) active
       dry yeast
1 1/2 teaspoons (7 ml) sugar
  3/4 teaspoon (3 ml) salt
    2 to 2 1/2 cups (500 to 625 ml)
       all-purpose flour
    1 egg yolk
    1 tablespoon (15 ml) water
       Coarse salt

Heat water to 120°F (48°C). Assemble Doughmaker. In large mixer bowl, combine 2 cups (500 ml) flour, yeast, sugar, salt, and warmed water. Mix with doughmaker at recommended speed for 3 minutes. (It may be necessary to scrape sides of bowl with rubber scraper and rotate bowl slightly by hand.) Add 2 cups (500 ml) flour and continue kneading for 3 minutes. If dough is sticky, knead in enough of remaining 1/2 cup (125 ml) flour to form a soft dough. Shape into a ball. On floured surface, cut into 16 pieces and roll with hands into approximately 12-inch (30 cm) ropes. Shape as pretzels and put onto foil-covered cookie sheets. Beat egg yolk and 1 tablespoon (15 ml) water with fork until well mixed. Brush egg mixture on dough to coat completely and sprinkle with salt. Bake in preheated 400°F (200°C) oven for 20 minutes. Remove from cookie sheets and cool on racks. Store in plastic bag or covered container no longer than 2 days.

16 pretzels

Cranberry Cheddar Bread

This flavor combination results in a mellow yet slightly tart bread.

    1 cup (250 ml) walnuts
    8 ounces (227 g) sharp Cheddar
       cheese, cut in 1-inch (2.5 cm)
       cubes and chilled
    3 cups (750 ml) all-purpose flour
    1 cup (250 ml) sugar
    2 teaspoons (10 ml) baking powder
1 1/2 teaspoons (7 ml) baking soda
  1/3 cup (75 ml) vegetable oil
    2 eggs
    1 can (16 ounces or 454 g)
       whole cranberry sauce

Preheat oven to 350°F (180°C). Assemble Blender. Put walnuts into blender container. Cover and process 2 cycles at WHIP to chop nuts; set aside. Cover blender container and set at BLEND. With motor running, remove feeder cap and drop 1 cup (250 ml) cheese cubes into container. Empty container. Repeat with remaining cheese. Assemble Mixer. In large mixer bowl put all remaining ingredients and cheese. Mix at LOW until dry ingredients are moistened then at MEDIUM-LOW until well combined. Divide equally in 2 greased 8 1/2×4 1/2×2 5/8-inch (22× 11×7 cm) loaf pans. Bake in preheated oven for 45 to 50 minutes, or until toothpick inserted in center comes out clean. Let cool completely before removing from pans.

2 loaves

The Cocktail Party

Whether you most enjoy quiet dinners or big celebrations, appetizers and drinks set the party mood. Either way, the Oster "Kitchen Center" appliance enables you to entertain with ease — with the elegance of pâtés and steak tartare, the informality of cheese balls and dips, the festivity of sparkling punches and frothy mixed drinks.

The "Kitchen Center" appliance allows you to plan a party according to the occasion rather than the amount of time you have for preparation. Appetizers as exquisite as Cocktail Cream Puffs are as easy to make as Creamy Dill Dip. You'll also find the do-ahead scheduling of Frosted Liver and Sausage Loaf just what you need to spend even more time with guests. For classic cocktails like Daiquiris and Piña Coladas, you need only turn on the "Osterizer" Blender at party time. And don't overlook the sure success of Milk Shakes, Malts and fresh fruit drinks for youngsters and the young-at-heart!

Liver Pâté

Combining liver, eggs, and seasonings will result in an impressive appetizer as well as a sandwich spread for rye bread.

   1 **pound (454 g) beef liver**
   1 **pound (454 g) chicken livers**
   2 **hard-cooked eggs, halved**
   2 **tablespoons (30 ml) light cream or**
1/2 **teaspoon (2 ml) garlic powder**
1/2 **teaspoon (2 ml) onion powder**
   1 **teaspoon (5 ml) salt**
1/2 **teaspoon (2 ml) pepper**

Put livers into saucepan and cover with water. Bring to a boil over high heat. Reduce heat to medium and simmer covered for 20 minutes, or until liver is cooked. Drain and cool thoroughly. Assemble Food Grinder with Fine Disc. Grind the liver and eggs into large bowl. Add remaining ingredients and mix well. Chill thoroughly before serving.

3 cups (750 ml) pâté

Saucy Cocktail Sausages

You will enjoy making your own cocktail sausages but when time is short, prepare this sauce for packaged cocktail sausages.

      24 Cocktail Sausages (page 78)
       1 can (15 ounces or 425 g)
              tomato sauce
       2 small onions, quartered
       3 drops hot pepper sauce
       1 teaspoon (5 ml) dry mustard
    1/2 teaspoon (2 ml) salt
    1/4 teaspoon (1 ml) pepper
    1/2 teaspoon (2 ml) ground allspice

Preheat oven to 350°F (180°C). Put sausages into an 8×8×2-inch (20×20×5 cm) baking pan and bake for 15 minutes. Turn sausages and continue baking for 15 minutes, or until thoroughly cooked. Assemble Blender. Put remaining ingredients into blender container. Cover and process at CHOP until onion is finely chopped. Pour into medium saucepan. Add sausages and simmer over low heat for 15 to 20 minutes. Serve hot in chafing dish with cocktail forks or toothpicks.

24 appetizers

Creamy Dill Dip

This sour cream dip is especially good with raw vegetables.

       1 cup (250 ml) dairy sour cream
    1/4 cup (50 ml) Blender Mayonnaise
              (page 97)
       1 tablespoon (15 ml) dill weed
    1 1/2 teaspoons (7 ml) dried
              parsley flakes
    1 1/4 teaspoons (6 ml) celery salt
    1/4 teaspoon (1 ml) onion powder
       1 clove garlic, mashed
    1/2 teaspoon (2 ml) prepared horseradish

Assemble Mixer. In small mixer bowl, put all ingredients and mix at LOW then at MEDIUM-LOW until smooth. Cover and chill at least 2 hours. Serve with raw vegetables such as carrot or celery sticks, cauliflower slices, and cherry tomatoes.

1 1/3 cups (325 ml) dip

Seasoned Steak Tartare

This cold canapé is a favorite of beef lovers everywhere.

       2 pounds (907 g) fresh lean beef
              sirloin steak or tenderloin
       4 anchovy fillets
       1 medium onion, quartered
       2 egg yolks
       1 teaspoon (5 ml) capers
       3 sprigs parsley, stems removed
       1 teaspoon (5 ml) Worcestershire sauce
    1/2 teaspoon (2 ml) freshly ground pepper
              Party rye or pumpernickel or
              assorted crackers

Assemble Food Grinder with Fine Disc. Trim all fat from steak; grind steak. Assemble Blender. Put remaining ingredients except bread into blender container. Cover and process at MIX until all ingredients are blended and chopped. Combine with meat. Cover and refrigerate until ready to serve. Just before serving, spread meat mixture on bread. If desired, serve extra chopped onion, salt, and pepper on the side.

32 servings

Note: Because the ingredients are to be eaten uncooked, special care should be taken in handling and keeping ingredients fresh, cold, and clean.

Frosted Liver and Sausage Loaf

Smooth cream cheese frosting and a well-seasoned pâté loaf make a dramatic appetizer.

    1   pound (454 g) chicken livers
    1/2 pound (227 g) Old-World Italian
          Sausage (page 116)
    1   small onion, quartered
    1/4 cup (50 ml) milk
    1/2 teaspoon (2 ml) salt
    1/2 teaspoon (2 ml) ground nutmeg
    2   tablespoons (30 ml) bourbon

Frosting:

    1   package (8 ounces or 227 g) cream
          cheese, at room temperature
    1   package (3 ounces or 85 g) cream
          cheese, at room temperature
    2   tablespoons (30 ml) butter or
          margarine, at room temperature
    1/2 teaspoon (2 ml) milk
        Assorted crackers

Line the bottom and the sides of a 7 1/2×3 3/4×2 1/4-inch (19×10×6 cm) loaf pan with foil. Rinse chicken livers and pat dry; set aside. If sausage is in casing, remove it. Fry sausage in small skillet until it loses its pink color. Remove sausage with slotted spoon and set aside. Cook chicken livers in sausage drippings until liver loses its pinkness. Assemble Blender. Put onion, milk, seasonings, and bourbon into blender container. Cover and process at GRIND. While blender is running, remove feeder cap and gradually add sausage, liver, and drippings to blender container. Process until smooth; mixture will be thick. (If necessary, STOP BLENDER, use rubber spatula to keep mixture around processing blades. Cover and continue to process.) Pour into prepared pan and refrigerate until set (8 to 12 hours). For Frosting, assemble Mixer. In small mixer bowl, put frosting ingredients and mix at MEDIUM-LOW until well blended and smooth. Loosen loaf and unmold on serving dish. Carefully remove foil. Frost sides and top with cream cheese mixture, garnish as desired. Return to refrigerator to set frosting. Serve with assorted crackers.

About 3 cups (750 ml) spread

Chili Cheese Ball

Four cheeses and fresh garlic are blended in this chili powder coated appetizer ball.

    8   ounces (227 g) Cheddar cheese,
          cubed
    2   ounces (57 g) blue or
          Roquefort cheese
    1   jar (5 ounces or 142 g) pasteurized
          process sharp Cheddar
          cheese spread
    1   package (3 ounces or 85 g) cream
          cheese, at room temperature
    1   clove garlic, minced
        Chili powder or paprika
        Assorted crackers

Assemble Food Grinder with Fine Disc. Alternately grind Cheddar and blue cheese into small mixer bowl. Assemble Mixer. Add cheese spread, cream cheese, and garlic to bowl with ground cheese. Mix at MEDIUM-LOW until well mixed. Form into one or two balls, wrap in waxed paper, and chill until easy to handle. Roll cheese ball in chili powder to coat. Accompany with assorted crackers.

About 2 cups (500 ml) spread

Dried Beef Roll-Ups

Horseradish adds zip to these appetizer roll-ups.

    2 packages (3 ounces or 85 g each)
        cream cheese, at room temperature
    2 teaspoons (10 ml) bottled
        horseradish sauce
    1 teaspoon (5 ml) grated onion
    1 teaspoon (5 ml) soy sauce
    2 tablespoons (30 ml) white wine
    1 jar (5 ounces or 142 g) sliced
        dried beef

Assemble Mixer. Add all ingredients except beef and mix at LOW then MEDIUM-LOW until well mixed. Spread about 1 teaspoon (5 ml) cheese mixture on each slice of beef and roll up. Put into pan and cover. Chill thoroughly. Before serving, slice each roll into thirds and secure with toothpicks.

102 appetizers

Cocktail Cream Puffs

Impress your guests with this beautiful appetizer complete with filling suggestions.

    1 cup (250 ml) water
    1/2 cup (125 ml) butter
    1/4 teaspoon (1 ml) salt
    1 cup (250 ml) all-purpose flour
    4 eggs
        Chicken 'n' Walnut Filling (opposite)
        or Spicy Salmon Filling (page 78)

Position top rack of oven just above the center. Preheat oven to 400°F (200°C). Put water, butter, and salt into small saucepan and bring to a boil over high heat (butter must be melted). Assemble Mixer. Rinse small mixer bowl with hot water; dry. Put flour and hot water-butter mixture into it. Mix at LOW then at MEDIUM-LOW until dough begins to ball around beaters. Add eggs, one at a time, mixing thoroughly at MEDIUM-LOW after each addition. Drop by tablespoonfuls onto a greased cookie sheet. Bake in preheated oven for 20 to 25 minutes, or until puffs are golden brown. Repeat procedure for remaining dough. Cool thoroughly before filling. To complete appetizers, carefully slice off tops of puffs, fill, and replace tops.

30 appetizers

Chicken 'n' Walnut Filling

The crunchiness of nuts adds a certain something to this appetizer puff filling.

    1 whole chicken breast (about 1 pound
        or 454 g) cooked, boned, and cut
        in 1-inch (2.5 cm) cubes
    1 cup (250 ml) walnuts
    1/2 cup (125 ml) Blender Mayonnaise
        (page 97)
    2 tablespoons (30 ml) light cream
    1/2 teaspoon (2 ml) salt
    1/4 teaspoon (1 ml) pepper

Assemble Food Grinder with Coarse Disc. Grind chicken (about 2 cups or 500 ml) and walnuts into small mixer bowl. Add remaining ingredients and mix well with spoon. Chill thoroughly before filling puffs.

About 2 1/2 cups (625 ml) filling

Spicy Salmon Filling

Salmon combines well with horseradish and sour cream in this appetizer puff filling.

    1/2 cup (125 ml) dairy sour cream
      1 package (3 ounces or 85 g) cream
           cheese, at room temperature
      2 tablespoons (30 ml) bottled
           horseradish sauce
    1/2 teaspoon (2 ml) freshly
           ground pepper
      1 can (15 1/2 ounces or 439 g)
           salmon, drained

Assemble Mixer. In small mixer bowl, mix sour cream, cream cheese, horseradish sauce, and pepper at LOW then at MEDIUM-HIGH until smooth. Add salmon and mix at LOW just until combined. Chill thoroughly before filling puffs.

2 cups (500 ml) filling

Beef Cheese Ball

Invite some friends in to enjoy this salty cheese ball served with assorted crackers.

    1/2 cup (125 ml) dry roasted peanuts
      1 jar (5 ounces or 142 g) sliced
           dried beef*
      1 medium onion, quartered
      1 package (8 ounces or 227 g) cream
           cheese, at room temperature
      1 tablespoon (15 ml) bottled
           horseradish sauce
      3 drops hot pepper sauce

Put peanuts into "Mini-Blend" container and process 3 cycles at GRIND to coarsely chop nuts; set aside. Assemble Food Grinder with Fine Disc and large mixer bowl. Grind beef and onion. Assemble Mixer. Add remaining ingredients except nuts and mix at LOW until blended. Shape mixture into a ball and roll in nuts to coat. Put onto serving plate and cover with plastic wrap. Chill for 4 hours before serving.

*One cup diced cooked roast beef may be substituted for dried beef.

1 cheese ball, 1 pound (454 g)

Cocktail Sausages

A mildly seasoned sausage to use for appetizers or in entrées.

           Sausage casing (sheep)
      1 pound (454 g) boneless beef chuck,
           cut in 1-inch (2.5 cm) pieces
      1 pound (454 g) boneless pork shoulder,
           cut in 1-inch (2.5 cm) pieces
      1 teaspoon (5 ml) salt
    1/2 teaspoon (2 ml) pepper
      1 teaspoon (5 ml) dry mustard
      1 teaspoon (5 ml) ground ginger

Prepare sausage casing. Assemble Food Grinder with Fine Disc. Grind beef and pork into large mixer bowl. Combine seasonings and mix with meat. Reassemble food grinder with Small Stuffing Tube. Stuff meat into casing. Twist or tie into 24 links. Chill thoroughly before separating links.

24 sausages

Note: To cook sausages, see baking directions in Saucy Cocktail Sausages on page 74, or brown and cook sausages in a skillet.

Crab Stuffed Cherry Tomatoes

These tomatoes are pretty to look at and yummy to eat.

- 1/2 medium green pepper, seeded and halved
- 1 tablespoon (15 ml) instant minced onion
- 1 can (6 1/2 ounces or 184 g) white crab meat
- 1/2 teaspoon (2 ml) soy sauce
- 1/2 cup (125 ml) dairy sour cream
- 30 cherry tomatoes, tops removed and seeded

Assemble Salad Maker with French Fry Cutter Disc and small mixer bowl. Process green pepper. Add remaining ingredients except tomatoes. Assemble Mixer. Mix at LOW then at MEDIUM-LOW until well combined. Cover bowl and chill for 2 hours. Fill each tomato with about 1 teaspoon (5 ml) chilled crab mixture. Arrange on serving platter and keep refrigerated until ready to serve.

30 appetizers

Mock Sour Cream

Higher in protein, lower in calories, and just as good as sour cream!

- 1/3 cup (75 ml) milk
- 1 tablespoon (15 ml) lemon juice
- 1 cup (250 ml) creamed cottage cheese

Assemble Blender. Put ingredients into blender container. Cover and process at BLEND until smooth and creamy.

1 cup (250 ml)

Ham Pineapple Ball

Increase the recipe and shape into one or more balls to serve a large group.

- 1 package (8 ounces or 227 g) cream cheese, at room temperature
- 1 can (4 1/2 ounces or 113 g) deviled ham
- 1/2 cup (125 ml) drained crushed pineapple
- 2 teaspoons (10 ml) prepared mustard
  Chopped chives (fresh or frozen)
  Assorted crackers

Assemble Mixer. In small mixer bowl, mix all ingredients except chives and crackers at LOW then at MEDIUM-LOW until well blended. Turn mixture onto square of foil, wrap, and chill until easy to handle. Form into a ball and cover generously with chives. Chill until ready to serve. Accompany with assorted crackers.

1 cup (250 ml) spread

Fruited Iced Tea

Be refreshed with a tall glass of this citrus tea.

- 1 large orange
- 1 lime
- 4 to 6 teaspoons (20 to 30 ml) instant tea
- 1 quart (1 liter) cold water
- 2 tablespoons (30 ml) honey

Assemble Citrus Juicer. Juice orange and lime into glass measure (about 1/2 cup or 125 ml orange juice and 2 tablespoons or 30 ml lime juice). Assemble Blender. Put juice and remaining ingredients into blender container. Cover and process at GRATE until well mixed. Pour into tall glasses filled with crushed ice.

5 servings

Curried Party Dip

Colorful vegetables in slices, chunks, and pieces are the dippers.

    1 cup (250 ml) Blender Mayonnaise
       (page 97)
    1 teaspoon (5 ml) curry powder
    1 teaspoon (5 ml) garlic salt
    1 teaspoon (5 ml) prepared horseradish
    1 teaspoon (5 ml) onion juice
    1 teaspoon (5 ml) vinegar

Assemble Blender. Put all ingredients into blender container. Cover and process at MIX, until smooth. (If necessary, STOP BLEND, use rubber spatula to keep mixture around processing blades. Cover and continue to process.) Serve with sliced cauliflower, cucumber, zucchini, celery, carrots, pepper chunks, and cherry tomatoes.

1 cup (250 ml) dip

Spicy Meatballs

Grinding the meat yourself for this recipe can be a real saving. Spice it up and you have an elegant party appetizer.

    1 pound (454 g) boneless beef chuck,
       cut in 1-inch (2.5 cm) pieces
    1 clove garlic
    1 medium onion, quartered
    1 slice bread, torn in pieces
    1 egg
    1 tablespoon (15 ml) soy sauce
  1/2 teaspoon (2 ml) ground ginger
  1/4 teaspoon (1 ml) ground allspice
  1/4 teaspoon (1 ml) ground red pepper or
       cayenne pepper
    1 can (10 1/2 ounces or 298 g) condensed
       beef broth
  1/2 teaspoon (2 ml) caraway seed
    2 tablespoons (30 ml) cornstarch
  1/4 cup (50 ml) water

Assemble Food Grinder with Fine Disc. Grind beef, garlic, onion, and bread into large mixer bowl. Mix egg, soy sauce, ginger, allspice, and red pepper with meat. Shape into 24 walnut-size balls and arrange on a foil-lined baking sheet. Bake at 350°F (180°C) for 30 minutes. Bring broth and caraway to a boil in medium saucepan. Dissolve cornstarch in water and add to broth slowly, stirring constantly. Reduce heat to warm. Remove the meatballs from baking sheet and put into sauce. Keep warm while serving. Serve with toothpicks or cocktail forks.

24 appetizers

Italian Sausage Pineapple Bake

This can be prepared using either home-made or store-bought sausage.

  2 1/4 pounds (1 kg) Italian sausages or
         or Old-World Italian Sausage
         (page 116)
      1 can (20 ounces or 566 g)
         pineapple chunks, juice reserved
      1 small onion, quartered
    1/4 cup (50 ml) soy sauce

Put Italian sausages into a 13×9×2-inch (33×23×5 cm) baking pan. Bake at 350°F (180°C) for 45 minutes. Cut sausages into bite-size pieces, 6 pieces per sausage. Return to pan. Assemble Blender. Drain pineapple juice (3/4 cup or 200 ml) into blender container. Add remaining ingredients except pineapple chunks. Cover and process at CHOP until onion is finely chopped. Add pineapple chunks to sausage and pour sauce into the pan. Cover tightly with foil. Bake at 350°F (180°C) for 20 minutes.

About 4 dozen appetizers

Sausage Biscuits

A spicy pizza-flavored snack that whets your appetite for more.

- 1/2 **pound (227 g) boneless pork shoulder, cut into 1-inch (2.5 cm) pieces**
- 1/2 **teaspoon (2 ml) salt**
- 1/4 **teaspoon (1 ml) pepper**
- 1/2 **teaspoon (2 ml) fennel seed**
- 1 **teaspoon (5 ml) dried Italian seasoning**
- 2 **cups (500 ml) biscuit mix**
- 1/2 **cup (125 ml) cold water**
  Pizza sauce, heated

Preheat oven to 400°F (200°C). Assemble Food Grinder with Fine Disc. Toss pork with salt, pepper, fennel seed, and Italian seasoning. Grind into large mixer bowl. Add biscuit mix and water; mix well. Drop by teaspoonfuls onto greased cookie sheets. Bake in preheated oven for 10 to 12 minutes, or until slightly brown. Remove from cookie sheets and serve hot with pizza sauce for dipping.

About 4 dozen appetizers

Piña Colada

This refreshing pineapple-rum drink is reminiscent of Old San Juan.

- 1/4 **cup (50 ml) cream of coconut**
- 1/2 **cup (125 ml) unsweetened pineapple juice**
- 2 **jiggers light or dark rum**
- 4 **or 5 ice cubes**

Assemble Blender. Put all ingredients into blender container. Cover and process at LIQUEFY until ice cubes are crushed. Pour over ice; garnish with a cherry and pineapple slice.

3 6-ounce (200 ml each) servings

Daiquiri

This is a quick version of a popular cocktail.

- 1/3 **cup (75 ml) frozen limeade concentrate, thawed**
- 3 **jiggers light rum**
- 5 **ice cubes**

Assemble Blender. Put all ingredients into blender container. Cover and process at LIQUEFY for a few seconds. Strain into cocktail glasses and serve.

2 6-ounce (200 ml each) servings

Frozen Daiquiri: Follow recipe for Daiquiri. Increase rum to 4 jiggers, double the amount of ice, and continue to blend until sherbet consistency. Do not strain.

4 6-ounce (200 ml each) servings

Tom and Jerry

A cold weather warm-up made easy in the blender.

- 2 **eggs**
- 2 **to 3 tablespoons (30 to 45 ml) sugar**
- 1/4 **cup (50 ml) dark rum**
- 1/2 **to 1 cup (125 to 250 ml) rye or bourbon**
  Dash ground cinnamon (if desired)
  Dash ground cloves (if desired)
- 1 1/2 **cups (375 ml) hot milk**
  Nutmeg

Assemble Blender. Put all ingredients except milk into blender container. Cover and process at WHIP until frothy and light yellow in color. With motor running remove feeder cap and add hot milk. Pour into warm mugs and sprinkle with ground nutmeg, if desired.

4 servings

Brandy Alexander Frappé

The favorite cocktail of ice cream fans.

> 1 **jigger brandy**
> 1 **jigger crème de cacao**
> 1/2 **cup (125 ml) milk**
> 1 **quart (1 liter) vanilla ice cream**

Assemble Blender. Put all ingredients into blender container. Cover and process at LIQUEFY until smooth.

4 6-ounce (200 ml each) servings

Variations: Substitute the following liqueurs for the brandy and crème de cacao:

Grasshopper
1 jigger white crème de cacao
1 jigger green crème de menthe

Golden Cadillac
1/2 jigger Galliano
1 1/2 jiggers white crème de cacao

Pink Squirrel
1 jigger crème de noyaux
1 jigger white crème de cacao

Koala Bear
1 jigger white crème de cacao
1 jigger coffee-flavored liqueur

Banana Buttermilk

This is a tart-sweet beverage.

> 1 **cup (250 ml) buttermilk, chilled**
> 1 **ripe banana**
> 1 **teaspoon (5 ml) honey**

Assemble Blender. Put all ingredients into blender container. Cover and process at LIQUEFY until smooth.

1 serving

Bunny Hop

Carrot lovers will enjoy the lively color and flavor of this drink.

> 1 **pound (454 g) carrots**
> 1/4 **medium pineapple, rind removed**

Assemble Juice Extractor. Process carrots and pineapple at recommended speed. Serve immediately.

1 serving

Brandied Slush

A do-ahead party beverage to keep on hand for unexpected company.

> 1 **cup (250 ml) water**
> 2 **tea bags**
> 2 **cups (500 ml) Hawaiian punch**
> 1 **lemon, quartered and seeded**
> 2/3 **cup (150 ml) sugar**
> 1 **cup (250 ml) brandy**
> **Club soda**

Heat water to a boil and add tea bags. Let steep for 5 minutes and remove bags. Assemble Blender. Pour tea and remaining ingredients except brandy and club soda into blender container. Cover and process at CHOP until lemon is very finely chopped. Pour into a 1 1/2-quart (1.5 liter) freezer container; stir in brandy. Cover and freeze for 3 to 4 days, or until sherbet consistency. To serve, fill an 8-ounce (250 ml) old-fashioned or high-ball glass half full of slush and add club soda to fill the glass.

24 servings

Banana Daiquiri

This cocktail is a mellow combination of bananas and rum.

- **1 lemon**
- **2 bananas, broken in 4 pieces each**
- **3 tablespoons (45 ml) sugar**
- **3 jiggers light rum**
- **6 ice cubes**

Assemble Citrus Juicer. Juice lemon into glass (about 1/4 cup or 50 ml). Assemble Blender. Pour lemon juice and remaining ingredients into blender container. Cover and process at LIQUEFY until smooth. Strain into cocktail glasses and serve.

4 6-ounce (200 ml each) servings

Frozen Banana Daiquiri: Follow recipe for Banana Daiquiri. Increase rum to 4 jiggers, double the amount of ice, and continue to blend until sherbet consistency.

6 6-ounce (200 ml each) servings

Party Punch

This wonderful punch can be prepared as needed to suit the size of your party

- **2 cups (500 ml) pineapple juice**
- **1 1/2 cups (375 ml) cranberry juice cocktail**
- **1/2 cup (125 ml) light rum**
- **1 lemon, peeled, quartered, and seeded**
- **1 quart (1 liter) ginger ale, chilled**
- **Red food coloring**

Assemble Blender. Put all ingredients except ginger ale and food coloring into blender container. Cover and process 2 cycles at MIX until lemon is finely chopped. Pour into a punch bowl and add ginger ale. Stir in food coloring, a drop at a time, to desired color.

18 4-ounce (125 ml each) servings

Peach Daiquiri

Tart yet delightfully pleasing.

- **1 lime**
- **1 ripe peach, peeled, quartered, and pitted**
- **3 tablespoons (45 ml) sugar**
- **2 dashes bitters**
- **3 jiggers light rum**
- **6 ice cubes**

Assemble Citrus Juicer. Juice lime into glass measure (about 2 tablespoons or 30 ml). Assemble Blender. Pour lime juice and remaining ingredients into blender container. Cover and process at LIQUEFY until smooth.

3 6-ounce (200 ml each) servings

Frozen Peach Daiquiri: Follow recipe for Peach Daiquiri. Increase rum to 4 jiggers, double the amount of ice, and continue to blend until sherbet consistency.

5 6-ounce (200 ml each) servings

Bacardi

This cocktail is named for the rum used.

- **1/3 cup (75 ml) frozen limeade concentrate, thawed**
- **4 jiggers light Bacardi rum**
- **1 1/2 cups (375 ml) crushed ice or 6 whole cubes**
- **3 tablespoons (45 ml) grenadine**

Assemble Blender. Put all ingredients into blender container. Cover and process at LIQUEFY a few seconds. Strain into cocktail glasses.

4 3-ounce (75 ml each) servings

Strawberry Rum Fizz

The preparation of this cocktail is made easy with the use of strawberry syrup.

    6 juice oranges
    2 large lemons
1 1/2 cups (375 ml) bottled strawberry
        syrup
      Red food coloring, optional
      Rum (about 1 1/4 cups or 300 ml)
    1 quart (1 liter) club soda or
        ginger ale, chilled

Assemble Citrus Juicer. Juice oranges and lemons (about 2 1/2 cups or 625 ml) orange juice and about 3/4 cup or 200 ml lemon juice). Stir in strawberry syrup and, if desired, food coloring. Chill. To serve, pour about 1/2 cup (125 ml) chilled mixture into each 8-ounce (250 ml) glass; add about 2 tablespoons (30 ml) rum and desired amount of crushed ice. Fill with club soda; stir.

9 or 10 servings

Milk Shakes and Malts

Many variations are possible by changing the flavor of ice cream and the flavoring.

    1 cup (250 ml) milk
    2 cups (500 ml) vanilla ice cream
      Flavoring
      Malted milk powder (if desired)

Assemble Blender. Put all ingredients into blender container. Cover and process at LIQUEFY until smooth.

2 8-ounce (250 ml each) servings

Pineapple Fizz

This fruit-flavored drink is a refreshing thirst-quencher.

    2 cups (500 ml) unsweetened
        pineapple juice
    1 can (12 ounces or 375 ml)
        apricot nectar
    1 cup (250 ml) pineapple sherbet
    1 bottle (10 ounces or 300 ml)
        club soda

Assemble Blender. Put pineapple juice, nectar, and sherbet into blender container. Cover and process at MIX until mixture is smooth. Pour into pitcher. Stir in club soda and pour immediately into glasses filled with crushed ice.

6 servings

Honey 'n' Fruit Drink

When peaches are in season, this drink will quench your thirst.

    2 large oranges
    1 ripe peach, peeled, pitted, and
        quartered
1/2 cup (125 ml) unsweetened
        pineapple juice
    2 tablespoons (30 ml) honey
    1 container (8 ounces or 227 g)
        plain yogurt

Assemble Citrus Juicer. Juice oranges into glass measure (about 3/4 cup or 200 ml). Assemble Blender. Put orange juice and remaining ingredients into blender container. Cover and process at LIQUEFY until smooth. Serve in glasses filled with crushed ice.

6 servings

Tossed and Sauced

An exciting cabbage? Fascinating carrots? A pepper with pizzazz? You won't believe it until you introduce the produce section of your supermarket to the precision slicing, shredding, and chopping power of the Oster "Kitchen Center" appliance. Then you'll discover the garden of creativity that's yours to harvest with whatever salad-makings the season provides.

Take the Vegetable Salad Bar concept and vary it according to what's available at your supermarket — with thinly sliced turnips, cauliflower, red cabbage, or other seasonal bargains. Highlight the lovely color of beets by shredding them in a salad counterpoint with hard-cooked egg. Stud a Holiday Gelatin Mold with the gemlike colors of ground cranberries, apples, and celery.

Or indulge a passion for salads with the main-course abundance of Taco Salad, Reuben Salad, or Overnight Layered Salad. Dressings to match the greenery? You'll find a dozen carefree blends in this chapter to mix and match with your salad favorites.

Julienne Beet Salad

A colorful salad to serve at a buffet.

- 1 **hard-cooked egg, peeled**
- 1 **pound (454 g) beets, cooked, peeled, and chilled**
- 1/2 **cup Red Wine Vinaigrette Dressing (page 97)**
- 8 **sprigs parsley, stems removed**
  Boston lettuce

Assemble Salad Maker with Shredder Disc and large bowl. Process egg; set in refrigerator. Cut beets into pieces to fit hopper. Process beets into bowl (about 2 cups or 500 ml). Mix dressing with beets. Chill for at least 1 hour. Put parsley into "Mini-Blend" container and process 3 cycles at STIR to chop parsley. Mix parsley with egg; set aside. Arrange lettuce in large salad bowl. With slotted spoon, drain beets and put onto lettuce. Sprinkle parsley-egg mixture over top.

6 servings

Special Cole Slaw

This is a definite do-ahead to have ready in the refrigerator.

> 1 medium head (about 2 pounds or 907 g) cabbage, cut in wedges
> 1 large green pepper, quartered and seeded
> 1 medium onion, halved
> 1 cup (250 ml) vinegar
> 2/3 cup (150 ml) vegetable oil
> 1 cup (250 ml) sugar
> 1 teaspoon (5 ml) salt
> 1 teaspoon (5 ml) celery seed
> 1/2 teaspoon (2 ml) dry mustard

Assemble Salad Maker with French Fry Cutter Disc and large bowl. Process cabbage, green pepper, and onion. Assemble Blender. Put remaining ingredients into blender container. Cover and process at BLEND until sugar is dissolved. Pour over cabbage and stir well. Cover and refrigerate up to 4 days.

8 to 10 servings

Blender Cole Slaw

This cole slaw is made with chopped cabbage.

> 3 cups (750 ml) cabbage pieces
> Seasoning
> Blender Mayonnaise (page 97) or other dressing

Assemble Blender. Put cabbage pieces into blender container. Cover with cold water. Cover and process 1 cycle at GRATE. (If a finer chop is desired, process 1 additional cycle.) Drain immediately through colander. Put into bowl and season to taste. Mix in desired amount of mayonnaise or other dressing.

1 1/2 cups (375 ml)

Summer Slaw

Small onion rings add interest to this version of cole slaw.

> 1 medium head (2 pounds or 907 g) cabbage, cut in wedges
> 4 small mild white onions
> 1/2 cup (125 ml) sugar
> 1/2 cup (125 ml) vinegar
> 1 teaspoon (5 ml) salt
> 1 teaspoon (5 ml) dry mustard
> 1 teaspoon (5 ml) celery seed
> 1/8 teaspoon (0.5 ml) pepper
> 1/2 cup (125 ml) vegetable oil
> Cherry tomato halves

Assemble Salad Maker with Thin Slicer Disc and large bowl. Process cabbage and onions. Stir to separate slices into rings, then mix lightly with cabbage. Combine all remaining ingredients except oil and tomatoes in saucepan. Bring to a boil, stirring until sugar is dissolved. Remove from heat; mix in oil and pour dressing over cabbage and onion. Let cool, then cover and chill for several hours or overnight; stir several times. Use slotted spoon to lift cabbage and onion from dressing to serving bowl. Garnish with cherry tomatoes.

6 to 8 servings

Avocado Dressing

> 1/3 cup (75 ml) milk
> 1 cup (250 ml) creamed cottage cheese
> 1 ripe avocado, peeled and cubed
> 3 drops hot pepper sauce
> Dash onion powder

Assemble Blender. Put all ingredients into blender container. Cover and process at BLEND until smooth.

1 1/2 cups (375 ml)

Celery Root Salad

A well-seasoned mayonnaise dressing coats delicately flavored celery root.

    1 firm celery root (1 1/2 to
          2 pounds or 681 to 907 g)
    3/4 cup (200 ml) Blender Mayonnaise
          (page 97)
    1 tablespoon (15 ml) dried onion flakes
    1 tablespoon (15 ml) lemon juice
    1 tablespoon (15 ml) light cream or
          half-and-half
    2 teaspoons (10 ml) prepared mustard
       Lettuce leaves

Assemble Salad Maker with Shredder Disc and large bowl. Wash celery root, cut into 1-inch (2.5 cm) slices, and pare slices. Process celery root. Prepare mayonnaise, then add remaining ingredients to blender container. Cover and process at BLEND just until mixed. Add to celery root and mix to coat. Chill for several hours. Arrange on lettuce in salad bowl. Sprinkle with paprika, if desired.

8 servings

Overnight Layered Salad

Spoon out salad in layers onto serving plates.

    1 head (1 to 1 1/4 pounds or 454 to
          565 g) iceberg lettuce, cut in wedges
    2 stalks celery, cut in 4-inch
          (10 cm) pieces
    1 small onion, halved
    2 carrots, pared
    1 package (10 ounces or 284 g)
          frozen peas, thawed
    3 hard-cooked eggs, halved
1 1/4 cups (300 ml) Blender Mayonnaise
          (page 97)
    2 tablespoons (30 ml) sugar
    4 slices bacon, crisp fried
          and crumbled

Assemble Salad Maker with Chunky Slicer Disc. Process lettuce into 4-quart (4 liter) bowl or dish. Change disc to Thin Slicer Disc and process celery and onion. Distribute evenly over lettuce. Change disc to Shredder Disc and process carrots; spread over celery and onion. Spread peas over carrots. Process eggs and sprinkle over peas and carrots. Mix mayonnaise and sugar and spread over entire top of salad (like frosting). Cover with foil or plastic wrap. Chill overnight. Before serving, remove cover and sprinkle with bacon.

8 to 10 servings

Cold Meat Salad

Ground cooked meat and fresh vegetable pieces are coated with a spicy mayonnaise dressing.

    1/2 pound (227 g) cold cooked beef,
          ham, or chicken
    1 large carrot, pared
    2 green onions, cut in pieces
    2 small sweet pickles
    2 ounces (57 g) Swiss cheese, cut
          in 1-inch (2.5 cm) cubes
    1/3 cup (75 ml) Blender Mayonnaise
          (page 97)
    1/2 teaspoon (2 ml) prepared horseradish
    1/2 teaspoon (2 ml) prepared mustard
       Dash salt and pepper
       Lettuce

Assemble Food Grinder with Coarse Disc. Grind meat, carrot, onion, pickles, and cheese into bowl. Mix mayonnaise, horseradish, mustard, salt, and pepper in small bowl. Stir dressing into meat mixture. Cover and chill for several hours. Arrange lettuce leaves on four plates. Spoon meat mixture evenly in four portions. Garnish with tomato wedges, if desired.

4 servings

Golden Salad

Carrot-cream cheese dressing coats apple and pineapple pieces in this unusual salad.

> 1 **can (20 ounces or 566 g) pineapple tidbits or chunks, drained**
> 2 **medium Golden Delicious apples, quartered and cored**
> 3 **medium carrots, pared**
> 1 **tablespoon (15 ml) lemon juice**
> 1 **package (3 ounces or 85 g) cream cheese, at room temperature, cut in pieces**
> 1/4 **teaspoon (1 ml) ground nutmeg**
> **Lettuce**

Assemble Salad Maker with French Fry Cutter Disc and large bowl. Process apples. Coat with lemon juice. Change disc to Shredder Disc; process carrots. Mix pineapple, apple, and carrot. Assemble Mixer. In small bowl, blend cream cheese, 1 tablespoon (15 ml) reserved pineapple syrup, and nutmeg on MEDIUM-LOW until smooth. Gently mix with apple mixture; chill. Serve on lettuce-lined plates or salad bowl.

6 servings

Celery Seed Dressing

This tangy dressing is fitting for both vegetable and fruit salads.

> 1 **cup (250 ml) vegetable oil**
> 1/2 **cup (125 ml) sugar**
> 1/3 **cup (75 ml) vinegar**
> 1 **tablespoon (15 ml) celery seed**
> 1 **teaspoon (5 ml) salt**
> 1 **teaspoon (5 ml) dry mustard**
> 2 **green onions, trimmed leaving some green top and cut in 1-inch (2.5 cm) pieces**

Assemble Blender. Put all ingredients into blender container. Cover and process at GRATE until onion is finely chopped. Chill thoroughly before serving. Shake well before pouring over salad.

1 2/3 cups (400 ml)

Pinto Beans with Sour Cream

A south-of-the-border salad that combines the tangy flavor of sour cream with the nutty flavor of beans.

> 1 **pound (454 g) dried pinto beans**
> 1 1/2 **quarts (1.5 liters) water**
> 2 1/2 **teaspoons (12 ml) salt**
> 1 **small onion, quartered**
> 4 **sprigs parsley, stems removed**
> 2/3 **cup (150 ml) sugar**
> 1 **teaspoon (5 ml) dry mustard**
> 1/4 **teaspoon (1 ml) pepper**
> 2 **hard-cooked eggs, halved**
> 1 **tablespoon (15 ml) vinegar**
> 1 **cup (250 ml) dairy sour cream**
> **Lettuce**

Rinse beans and put into Dutch oven or saucepan. Add water and bring rapidly to a boil; boil 2 minutes and remove from heat. Set aside covered for 1 hour. Add 2 teaspoons (10 ml) salt. Bring to a boil and simmer covered for 2 hours, or until beans are tender. Drain beans and chill thoroughly. Put beans into large bowl. Assemble Blender. Put 1/2 teaspoon (2 ml) salt and remaining ingredients except lettuce into blender container. Cover and process at LIQUEFY until well mixed. (If necessary, STOP BLENDER, use rubber spatula to keep mixture around processing blades. Cover and continue to process.) Pour over beans, mix well, and chill for 4 hours. Serve on a bed of lettuce.

10 to 12 servings

Cucumber Ring Mold

The tart flavor of lime points up the distinctive flavor of cucumber.

- 1 **large cucumber, pared, halved lengthwise, and seeded**
- 1 **small onion, halved**
- 1 **stalk celery, cut in 4-inch (10 cm) lengths**
- 1 **package (3 ounces or 85 g) lime-flavored gelatin**
- 1 1/4 **cups (300 ml) boiling water**
- 1 **tablespoon (15 ml) vinegar**
- 1/2 **teaspoon (2 ml) salt**
  Salad greens

Assemble Salad Maker with Thin Slicer Disc and large mixer bowl. Process cucumber, onion, and celery. Spread evenly in bottom of a 1-quart (1 liter) ring mold. Assemble Blender. Put remaining ingredients except greens into blender container. Cover, remove feeder cap, and process at MIX until gelatin is dissolved. Chill until slightly thickened. Pour gelatin over vegetables in mold. Chill until firm (about 4 hours). To unmold, dip bottom of mold in hot water, turn mold over on serving plate, and shake gently until gelatin drops from mold. Garnish with salad greens.

6 to 8 servings

Honey Dressing

This celery seed dressing is a good choice for fruit salads.

- 1 **cup (250 ml) vegetable oil**
- 2/3 **cup (150 ml) honey**
- 1/4 **cup (50 ml) vinegar**
- 1 **teaspoon (5 ml) celery seed**
- 1 **teaspoon (5 ml) dry mustard**
- 1 **teaspoon (5 ml) paprika**
- 1/4 **teaspoon (1 ml) salt**

Assemble Blender. Put all ingredients into blender container. Cover and process at MIX until honey is thoroughly mixed with oil. Serve at once or store in refrigerator. Shake well before serving.

1 2/3 cups (400 ml)

Holiday Gelatin Mold

Feeding a crowd for the holidays? This is a perfect do-ahead salad for those busy days.

- 3 **cups (750 ml) fresh whole cranberries**
- 4 **medium-size tart apples, quartered, pared and cored**
- 1 **stalk celery, cut in 4-inch (10 cm) lengths**
- 1 **can (20 ounces or 566 g) pineapple chunks, drained; reserve syrup**
- 1 **package (3 ounces or 85 g) orange-pineapple-flavored gelatin**
- 1 **package (3 ounces or 85 g) strawberry-flavored gelatin**
- 1 3/4 **cups (450 ml) boiling water**
  Orange juice
  Lettuce leaves

Assemble Food Grinder with Coarse Disc. Grind cranberries, apples, and celery into large mixer bowl. Mix in pineapple chunks. Spread evenly in a 13×9×2-inch (33×23×5 cm) pan. Assemble Blender. Empty gelatin packages into blender container and add boiling water. Cover and process at BEAT until gelatin is dissolved. Pour into large bowl. Add enough orange juice to the reserved pineapple syrup to make 2 cups (500 ml) liquid. Add to gelatin mixture and stir well. Pour gelatin over fruit in pan and stir just to mix. Chill until firm (about 5 hours). Cut into squares and serve on salad plates lined with lettuce leaves.

12 to 16 servings

German Potato Salad with Knockwurst

The sausage is mixed in with the sweet-sour potato salad in this version of a well-known German dish.

    2 to 2 1/2 pounds (907 to 1134 g)
         salad or new potatoes
    1 stalk celery
    1 small mild onion
    8 sprigs parsley, stems removed
1 1/2 pounds (681 g) knockwurst
    1 tablespoon (15 ml) vegetable oil
  1/4 cup (5 ml) sugar
    1 tablespoon (15 ml) all-purpose flour
    1 teaspoon (5 ml) salt
    1 teaspoon (5 ml) celery seed
    1 teaspoon (5 ml) dry mustard
  1/4 teaspoon (1 ml) paprika
  1/8 teaspoon (0.5 ml) pepper
    1 cup (250 ml) chicken broth
  1/2 cup (125 ml) vinegar

Cook potatoes with skins on. Peel when cool enough to handle; chill. Meanwhile, assemble Salad Maker with Thin Slicer Disc. Process celery then onion; set aside. Change disc to Thick or Chunky Slicer Disc and process potatoes; set aside. Put parsley into "Mini-Blend" container and process 5 cycles at BLEND to chop parsley; set aside. Remove and discard sausage casing; cut sausage into 1/4-inch (0.6 cm) slices. Put oil and knockwurst into a large skillet over medium heat; stir until lightly browned. Remove sausage with slotted spoon; set aside. Mix sugar, flour, salt, celery seed, dry mustard, paprika, and pepper; stir into drippings in skillet. Stir in broth and vinegar. Cook, stirring until dressing boils and thickens. Add potatoes, knockwurst, onion, celery, and 2 tablespoons (30 ml) chopped parsley to sauce; gently stir to coat pieces and heat thoroughly. Put into serving dish and sprinkle with remaining parsley. Serve warm.

6 to 8 servings

Taco Salad

The layers of the salad can best be seen in a straight-sided clear glass bowl.

    1 package (10 ounces or 284 g)
         corn chips
    1 pound (454 g) boneless beef chuck,
         cut into 1-inch (2.5 cm) pieces
    1 package (1.25 ounces or 35 g)
         taco seasoning mix
    1 head lettuce, cut in wedges
    1 green pepper, quartered and seeded
    1 small onion, halved
    6 ounces (170 g) Cheddar cheese, cut
         in 1-inch (2.5 cm) cubes and chilled
    1 tomato, diced
       Avocado Dressing (page 88)

Put 4 cups (1 liter) corn chips into a 4-quart (4 liter) bowl or 13×9-inch (33×23 cm) pan. Assemble Food Grinder with Fine Disc. Grind meat into bowl. Heat skillet, add meat, and brown lightly. Add taco mix, following directions on package. Set aside. Assemble Salad Maker with Chunky Slicer or Thick Slicer Disc. Process lettuce into bowl with corn chips. Change disc to French Fry Cutter Disc and process green pepper. Change disc to Thin Slicer Disc and process onion. Assemble Blender. Cover and remove feeder cap. Set at BLEND. With blender on, drop 1 cup (250 ml) cheese cubes into blender container. Add cheese to bowl. Repeat with remaining cheese for about 1 1/2 cups (375 ml). Add layers of taco beef mixture, diced tomato, and 1 cup (250 ml) corn chips. Serve with remaining corn chips and Avocado Dressing.

6 servings

Herbed Salad Dressing

Serve this dressing over your favorite salad greens.

- 1 cup (250 ml) vegetable oil
- 1/2 cup (125 ml) vinegar
- 1 sprig parsley, stems removed
- 1 teaspoon (5 ml) celery salt
- 1 teaspoon (5 ml) chervil
- 1 teaspoon (5 ml) fennel seed
- 1 teaspoon (5 ml) oregano leaves
- 1 teaspoon (5 ml) dry mustard
- 1/2 teaspoon (2 ml) pepper

Assemble Blender. Put all ingredients into blender container. Cover and process at MIX until well combined.

1 2/3 cups (400 ml)

Reuben Salad

This main dish salad has the makings of a Reuben sandwich.

- 1/3 cup (75 ml) ketchup
- 1/4 cup (50 ml) Blender Mayonnaise (page 97)
- 1 tablespoon (15 ml) prepared horseradish
- 1 teaspoon (5 ml) lemon juice
- 3 tablespoons (45 ml) butter or margarine
- 3 slices rye bread
- 6 ounces (170 g) Swiss cheese
- 1 small head iceberg lettuce, cut in wedges
- 1/2 pound (227 g) sliced cooked corned beef, rolled
- 1 can (8 ounces or 227 g) sauerkraut, drained

Mix ketchup, mayonnaise, horseradish, and lemon juice in bowl; set aside. Spread butter on both sides of bread. Heat large skillet and brown bread on both sides. Cut in 1/2-inch (1.3 cm) strips; set aside. Assemble Salad Maker with French Fry Cutter Disc and bowl. Process cheese; set aside. Change disc to Thick Slicer Disc. Process lettuce. Line large serving plate with lettuce. Put bowl of dressing in center. Arrange rolled corned beef slices, toasted bread strips, sauerkraut, and cheese around dressing.

4 to 6 servings

Greek Salad

Flavors of Greek cuisine come to life in this colorful salad.

- 1/2 green pepper, seeded and halved
- 1 medium onion, halved
- 2 stalks celery, cut in 4-inch (10 cm) lengths
- 10 jumbo pitted ripe olives
- 1/2 small head cauliflower, cut in flowerets
- 1 small head lettuce
- 3 Italian plum tomatoes, pared and cut in thin slices
- 2/3 cup (150 ml) olive oil
- 1/4 cup (50 ml) vinegar
- 1/4 cup (50 ml) lemon juice
- 8 sprigs fresh parsley, stems removed
- 1 teaspoon (5 ml) dried mint
- 7 ounces (198 g) feta cheese, crumbled or cut in pieces

Assemble Salad Maker with French Fry Cutter Disc and large bowl. Process green pepper and onion. Change disc to Thick Slicer Disc and process celery, olives, and cauliflower. In separate bowl process lettuce, set aside. Add tomatoes to bowl. Assemble Blender. Put oil, vinegar, lemon juice, parsley and mint into blender container. Cover and process at MIX until parsley is finely chopped. Pour dressing over vegetables and marinate covered in refrigerator for 3 hours. To serve, arrange a bed of lettuce on each plate. Spoon vegetables onto lettuce, top with cheese, and spoon dressing over all. Serve cold.

6 servings

Caper French Dressing

Serve on mixed salad greens.

    1/2 cup (125 ml) vegetable oil
    1/2 cup (125 ml) olive oil
    1/3 cup (75 ml) wine vinegar
      2 teaspoons (10 ml) sugar
1 1/2 teaspoons (7 ml) salt
    1/8 teaspoon (0.5 ml) white pepper
      2 tablespoons (30 ml) capers
      1 tablespoon (15 ml) caper juice
      1 small wedge onion (1/2 inch or
           1.3 cm)
1 1/2 teaspoons (7 ml) dry mustard
      1 teaspoon (5 ml) paprika

Assemble Blender. Put all ingredients into blender container. Cover and process at PUREE until capers are minced. Chill several hours before serving.

1 1/2 cups (375 ml)

Blender Mayonnaise

Use wherever mayonnaise is needed.

      1 egg
    1/2 teaspoon (2 ml) salt
    1/2 teaspoon (2 ml) sugar
    1/2 teaspoon (2 ml) dry mustard
           Dash red pepper
      2 tablespoons (30 ml) white
           tarragon vinegar
      1 cup (250 ml) vegetable oil

Assemble Blender. Put egg, seasonings, vinegar, and 1/4 cup (50 ml) oil into blender container. Cover and process at BLEND. Immediately remove feeder cap and pour in remaining oil in a steady stream. (If necessary, STOP BLENDER and use rubber spatula to keep mixture around processing blades. Cover and continue to process until smooth.) Store covered in refrigerator up to 1 week.

About 1 1/4 cups (300 ml)

Blue Cheese Buttermilk Dressing

Serve on tossed salad greens or mixed vegetable salads.

1 1/4 cups Blender Mayonnaise (page 97)
    1/2 cup (125 ml) buttermilk
      1 1/2-inch (1.3 cm) slice medium onion
      2 teaspoons (10 ml) Worcestershire
           sauce
    1/4 teaspoon (1 ml) garlic powder
      3 ounces (85 g) blue or Roquefort
           cheese, cut up

Assemble Blender. Put all ingredients except blue cheese into blender container. Cover and process at BLEND until smooth. (If necessary, STOP BLENDER, use rubber spatula to keep mixture around processing blades.) Add cheese, cover, and process at BLEND until cheese is chopped. Store in refrigerator.

2 1/2 cups (625 ml) dressing

Red Wine Vinaigrette Dressing

Use as a salad dressing or marinade for vegetables.

    3/4 cup (200 ml) olive oil, or 3
           tablespoons (45 ml) olive oil and
           vegetable oil to make 3/4 cup (200 ml)
    1/4 cup (50 ml) red wine vinegar
      1 small clove garlic, minced
      2 teaspoons (10 ml) prepared mustard
      1 teaspoon (5 ml) prepared horseradish
      1 teaspoon (5 ml) salt
           Dash freshly ground pepper

Assemble Blender. Put all ingredients into blender container. Cover and process at CHOP until mixed.

1 cup (250 ml)

Vegetable Salad Bar

Supply guests with chilled salad bowls or plates and let them "build" their own salads.

AMOUNT	DISC
3 carrots, pared	Shredder Disc
4 hard-cooked eggs	Shredder Disc
1 cucumber	Thin Slicer Disc
8 ounces (227 g) fresh mushrooms	Thin Slicer Disc
1 zucchini	French Fry Cutter Disc
1 head iceberg lettuce,	Thick Slicer Disc
3 stalks celery	Thick Slicer Disc
8 ounces (227 g) Cheddar, cut in 1-inch (2.5 cm) pieces	Blender Chop
8 ounces (227 g) crumbled bacon	
1 pint (500 ml) cherry tomatoes, rinsed	
2 cups (500 ml) alfalfa sprouts	
Blue Cheese Buttermilk Dressing (page 97)	
Red Wine Vinaigrette Dressing (page 97)	
Zesty Tomato French Dressing (opposite)	

Assemble Salad Maker with Shredder Disc. Process carrots and eggs into separate bowls; set aside. Change disc to Thin Slicer Disc and process cucumber and mushrooms into separate bowls; set aside. Change disc to French Fry Cutter Disc and process zucchini. Change disc to Thick Slicer Disc and process lettuce and celery into large bowl; set aside. Assemble Blender. Cover blender and set at BLEND. With motor on, remove feeder cap and drop 1 cup (250 ml) cheese cubes into container. Repeat wtih remaining cheese. Cover and refrigerate ingredients until time to serve. Put crumbled bacon, tomatoes, and alfalfa sprouts into separate bowls. Put lettuce into large salad bowl with all other ingredients in small appropriate bowls around lettuce. Each bowl should have a serving spoon. Salad dressing should be in easy-to-help-yourself containers with ladles.

10 to 12 servings

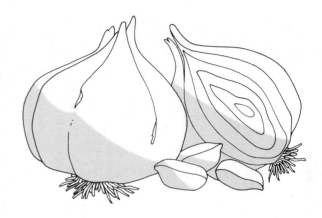

Zesty Tomato French Dressing

Serve this well-seasoned dressing on vegetable or seafood salads.

1	can (10 3/4 ounces or 305 g) condensed tomato soup
2/3	cup (150 ml) vinegar
1/2	cup (125 ml) vegetable oil
1	tablespoon (15 ml) Worcestershire sauce
2	teaspoons (10 ml) salt
1/4	teaspoon (1 ml) pepper
1	teaspoon (5 ml) prepared mustard
1/2	cup (125 ml) sugar
2	tablespoons (30 ml) prepared horseradish
1	small clove garlic,

Assemble Blender. Put all ingredients into blender container. Cover and process at BLEND until smooth. Store in refrigerator.

2 2/3 cups (700 ml) dressing

Blue Cheese Buttermilk Dressing (page 97), Zesty Tomato French Dressing, Red Wine Vinaigrette Dressing, Vegetable Salad Bar

Green Goddess Dressing

Serve this creamy dressing on mixed greens or seafood salad.

- 1 cup (250 ml) Blender Mayonnaise (page 97)
- 1 clove garlic, halved
- 2 green onions, cut in pieces
- 1 tablespoon (15 ml) anchovy paste
- 1/2 cup (125 ml) dairy sour cream
- 2 tablespoons (30 ml) tarragon vinegar
- 1/2 teaspoon (2 ml) sugar
- 1/2 teaspoon (2 ml) salt
- 1/8 teaspoon (0.5 ml) pepper
- 1 1/2 teaspoons (7 ml) lemon juice
- 1 sprig parsley, stems removed

Assemble Blender. Put all ingredients into blender container. Cover and process at MIX until onion is finely chopped. Serve chilled.

1 1/2 cups (375 ml)

Sweet and Sour Dressing

Combine green beans, tomatoes, and green pepper to make a salad for this dressing.

- 1/4 cup (50 ml) olive oil
- 2 tablespoons (30 ml) vinegar
- 1 tablespoon (15 ml) sugar
- 1 teaspoon (5 ml) salt
- 1/2 teaspoon (2 ml) pepper
- 1/4 small red onion
- 2 tablespoons (30 ml) chopped chives
- 1 sprig parsley, stems removed

Put all ingredients into "Mini-Blend" container and process 4 cycles at CHOP to chop onion.

3/4 cup (200 ml)

Spicy Salad Dressing

This spicy-hot salad dressing is especially good on tossed green salad.

- 1 3/4 cups (450 ml) vegetable oil
- 3/4 cup (200 ml) tarragon vinegar
- 1 small onion, quartered
- 1 whole bay leaf
- 1 teaspoon (5 ml) salt
- 1/2 teaspoon (2 ml) pepper
- 1 teaspoon (5 ml) chili powder
- 1/4 teaspoon (1 ml) ground red pepper or cayenne pepper

Assemble Blender. Put all ingredients into blender container. Cover and process at CHOP until onion and bay leaf are chopped.

2 1/2 cups (625 ml)

Seafood Cocktail Sauce

Your favorite seafood will taste extra special with this spicy sauce.

- 1/2 cup (125 ml) catsup
- 1/2 lemon, cut into pieces
- 1/2 tablespoon (7 ml) horseradish
- 1/4 cup (50 ml) chili sauce
- 1/2 teaspoon (2 ml) Worcestershire sauce

Put all ingredients into "Mini-Blend" container. Process at LIQUEFY until smooth. Serve with shrimp, oysters, lobster, or crab.

3/4 cup (200 ml)

What's For Dinner?

What would you *like* for dinner tonight? Crispy Barbecued Ribs, tender Home-Style Swiss Steak, or Chicken with Orange Sauce? Perhaps you would prefer Chinese-style Hong Kong Pork Chops or Italian Sausage and Eggplant. If you'd like fish, there's Baked Trout with Apple Stuffing or Haddock in Herb Sauce. And these are only a few possibilities!

You can savor a different cuisine every night of the week and enjoy meat-budget savings too with the Oster "Kitchen Center" appliance. You can buy extra quantities of beef, pork, ham, chicken, and turkey when the meats are on sale; then use the Food Grinder to turn reserved portions into a superb variety of homemade sausages, casseroles, and meat loaves, as well as stuffed peppers, cabbage, and zucchini. You can count on the "Osterizer" Blender to perk up plain baked or broiled meats with tangy Horseradish or Mustard Sauce. And when the occasion calls for something sublime, turn to the Doughmaker for luscious homemade Ravioli or Fettucini Pesto.

Hunter's Stew

An oven dinner to satisfy hearty appetites.

- 2 pounds (907 g) boneless beef chuck, cut in 2-inch (5 cm) pieces
- 2 large carrots, pared
- 4 medium potatoes, pared
- 1 medium onion, halved
- 1 teaspoon (5 ml) salt
- 1/2 teaspoon (2 ml) pepper
- 1 can (10 3/4 ounces or 305 g) condensed tomato soup
- 1/2 cup (125 ml) water

Assemble Food Grinder with Coarse Disc. Grind meat into a 9×9×2-inch (23×23×5 cm) baking pan. Assemble Salad Maker with Thick Slicer Disc and process carrots, potatoes, and onion into pan with meat. Mix salt, pepper, soup, and water and pour over meat and vegetables. Cover tightly with foil. Bake at 300°F (150°C) for 2 hours.

6 to 8 servings

Home-Style Swiss Steak

Fresh tomatoes and parsley are used in the sauce for these individual Swiss steaks.

2 1/2 pounds (1.25 kg) beef round
     steak
  2 tablespoons (30 ml) vegetable oil
1/2 cup (125 ml) all-purpose flour
  1 teaspoon (5 ml) salt
1/2 teaspoon (2 ml) pepper
  4 large tomatoes, peeled
  1 teaspoon (5 ml) dry mustard
  1 stalk celery, cut in 1-inch
     (2.5 cm) pieces
  1 small onion, quartered
  4 sprigs parsley, stems removed

Cut steak into portions, trimming fat and removing bone. Heat oil in skillet. Put flour, salt, and pepper into a flat dish and coat meat with flour. Brown meat on both sides in oil. Assemble Blender. Put remaining ingredients into blender container. Cover and process at LIQUEFY until finely chopped. Pour over steak and simmer covered for 1 1/2 hours, or until meat is tender and sauce is slightly thickened. Serve with rice.

4 to 6 servings

Italian Meatballs

  1 pound (454 g) boneless beef chuck,
     cut in 1-inch (2.5 cm) pieces
  4 slices white bread, torn in pieces
  4 sprigs parsley, stems removed
1/4 cup (50 ml) water
  2 eggs
1/4 cup (50 ml) grated Parmesan cheese
  1 teaspoon (5 ml) salt
1/4 teaspoon (1 ml) oregano
  2 tablespoons (30 ml) vegetable oil

Assemble Food Grinder with Fine Disc. Grind meat, bread, and parsley into large

bowl. Add remaining ingredients except oil and stir well to mix. Shape meat mixture into balls. Heat oil in a skillet, add meatballs, and brown on all sides. Use as directed.

24 meatballs

Mushroom Steaks

A budget stretcher!.

  1 pound (454 g) stew meat or
     chuck roast, cut in 1-inch
     (2.5 cm) pieces
  2 slices white bread
  1 small onion
1/4 green pepper
  1 clove garlic, minced
1/2 teaspoon (2 ml) dry mustard
1/2 teaspoon (2 ml) salt
1/2 teaspoon (2 ml) pepper

Assemble Food Grinder with Fine Disc. Grind meat, bread, onion, and green pepper alternating ingredients. Combine with seasonings. Shape into 6 patties, using 1/3 cup (75 ml) for each. Panfry over medium heat until brown, turn and cook other side.

Mushroom Sauce

1/2 small onion
1/4 pound (113 g) fresh mushrooms
  3 tablespoons (45 ml) butter or
     margarine
1 1/4 cups (300 ml) water
  3 tablespoons (45 ml) flour
  1 beef bouillon cube
1/4 teaspoon (1 ml) bottled
     browning sauce
     Dash pepper

Assemble Salad Maker with French Fry Cutter Disc and large bowl. Process onion and mushrooms. Move meat patties to one side of pan. Melt butter and sauté onion and mushrooms until tender. Assemble Blender. Place all remaining ingredients into blender container. Cover and process at BLEND. Pour over mushrooms. Stir and cook until thickened. Spoon over patties, cover and heat on low 10 minutes. Serve over buttered noodles.

6 servings

Special Meat Loaf

Horseradish is the special flavor in this beef and pork loaf.

  2 **pounds (907 g) boneless lean beef chuck, cut in 1-inch (2.5 cm) pieces**
1/2 **pound (227 g) boneless pork, cut in 1-inch (2.5 cm) pieces**
  1 **small onion, quartered**
  2 **slices white bread, torn in pieces**
  2 **eggs, slightly beaten**
  1 **cup (250 ml) milk**
  1 **tablespoon (15 ml) prepared horseradish**
  1 **teaspoon (5 ml) salt**
1/4 **teaspoon (1 ml) pepper**
  2 **slices bacon**

Assemble Food Grinder with Fine Disc. Grind beef, pork, onion, and bread into large bowl. Add remaining ingredients except bacon to bowl and mix until combined. Pack into a 9 1/4 × 5 1/4 × 2 3/4-inch (23 × 13 × 8 cm) loaf pan. Top with bacon slices. Bake at 350°F (180°C) for 1 1/2 hours, or until meat is well browned and shrinks from sides of pan.

8 servings

Oslo Meatballs

Norwegian meatballs are traditionally small and served in sauce.

  1 **pound (454 g) boneless beef chuck, cut in 1-inch (2.5 cm) pieces**
1/2 **pound (227 g) boneless pork shoulder, cut in 1-inch (2.5 cm) pieces**
  2 **slices bread, torn in pieces**
  1 **egg**
  1 **teaspoon (5 ml) salt**
1/4 **teaspoon (1 ml) pepper**
1/4 **teaspoon (1 ml) ground nutmeg**
      Medium White Sauce (page 106; double recipe)
1/2 **envelope (1.37-ounce or 38 g size) onion soup mix**
1/2 **cup (125 ml) dairy sour cream**

Assemble Food Grinder with Fine Disc and large bowl. Grind beef, pork, and bread. Add egg, salt, pepper, and nutmeg; mix well. Shape into walnut-size balls. Brown meatballs in hot skillet. When brown, remove meatballs with slotted spoon. Prepare white sauce in large saucepan. Stir in onion soup mix. Add meatballs to sauce and simmer covered 10 minutes. Just before serving, add sour cream and mix well.

6 to 8 servings

Beef with Caraway and Vegetables

This pot roast with sour cream sauce is accompanied by colorful carrot and zucchini slices.

        1   3-to 4-pound (1.5 to 2 kg)
              boneless beef bottom round roast
        2   cups (500 ml) beef broth
        1   cup (250 ml) dry sherry
        1   can (6 ounces or 170 g) tomato paste
        1   small onion, quartered
        1   stalk celery, cut in 1-inch
              (2.5 cm) pieces
      1/2   teaspoon (2 ml) thyme
        1   bay leaf
        2   tablespoons (30 ml) solid shortening
        2   teaspoons (10 ml) caraway seed
        3   to 4 carrots, pared
        3   small zucchini
        2   tablespoons (30 ml) vegetable
              oil
        1   cup (250 ml) dairy sour cream

Put roast into large mixing bowl. Assemble Blender. Put broth, sherry, tomato paste, onion, celery, thyme, and bay leaf into blender container. Cover and process at BEAT, until finely chopped. Pour over roast in bowl and cover with foil. Refrigerate for at least 12 hours. Drain roast well and reserve with marinade. Heat shortening in Dutch oven, add meat, and brown on all sides. Add marinade and caraway to Dutch oven; cover. Bake at 350°F (180°C) for 1 1/2 hours, or until meat is tender. Meanwhile, assemble Salad Maker with Crinkle Cut Slicer Disc and large bowl. Process carrots. Change disc to Chunky Slicer Disc. Process zucchini. Heat oil in skillet, add carrot and zucchini, and stir to coat. Cook covered over low heat, stirring occasionally, until vegetables are tender (about 15 minutes). When meat is tender, put roast on serving platter. Skim fat from pan liquid and stir in

sour cream with whisk. Serve in boat. Accompany roast with cooked vegetables and mashed potatoes.

6 to 8 servings

Chili Monterey Style

Freeze some of this chili to serve later.

        2   pounds (907 g) boneless beef chuck,
              cut in 1-inch (2.5 cm) pieces
        1   clove garlic
        2   large onions, quartered
      1/2   green pepper, seeded
        2   tablespoons (30 ml) vegetable oil
        3   tablespoons (45 ml) chili powder
        2   teaspoons (10 ml) ground cumin
        1   cup (250 ml) beef broth
        1   can (28 ounces or 793 g)
              tomatoes, undrained
        3   cans (16 ounces or 454 g) red kidney
              beans, undrained
        1   teaspoon (5 ml) salt
        1   cup (250 ml) uncooked spaghetti,
              broken in 1-inch (2.5 cm) pieces

Assemble Food Grinder with Fine Disc. Grind meat, garlic, onion, and green pepper into bowl. Heat oil in Dutch oven or saucepan over medium heat; sauté beef, onion, and green pepper. Add chili powder, cumin, beef broth, tomatoes, kidney beans, and salt. Simmer covered for 1 hour. Add spaghetti; simmer covered for 30 minutes.

8 to 10 servings

Stuffed Cabbage Leaves

This old-world favorite is sure to please.

- 1 pound (454 g) boneless veal shoulder, cut in 1-inch (2.5 cm) pieces
- 1 pound (454 g) boneless beef chuck, cut in 1-inch (2.5 cm) pieces
- 1 small onion, quartered
- 1 cup (250 ml) uncooked quick-cooking rice
- 1 teaspoon (5 ml) dill weed
- 1 teaspoon (5 ml) thyme
- 1 teaspoon (5 ml) salt
- 1/2 teaspoon (2 ml) pepper
- 12 large cabbage leaves
- 1 can (15 ounces or 425 g) tomato sauce

Assemble Food Grinder with Fine Disc. Grind veal, beef, and onion into large bowl. Add rice and seasonings; mix well. Rinse cabbage leaves and drop into boiling water for 1 minute, or until limp. Drain leaves and pat dry. Put about 1/2 cup (125 ml) meat mixture onto each leaf and fold envelope style. Put seam side down in greased 13×9×2-inch (33×23×5 cm) baking pan. Pour tomato sauce over cabbage rolls. Cover pan with foil. Bake at 350°F (180°C) for 45 minutes.

12 servings

Medium White Sauce

A basic sauce with thin and thick variations.

- 2 tablespoons (30 ml) butter, at room temperature
- 2 tablespoons (30 ml) all-purpose flour
- 1 cup (250 ml) milk or cream
- 1/4 teaspoon (1 ml) salt
- Dash pepper

Assemble Blender. Put ingredients into blender container. Cover and process at WHIP until well blended. Pour into saucepan and cook over low heat, stirring constantly until thick.

Thin White Sauce: Follow recipe for Medium White Sauce, reducing butter and flour to 1 tablespoon (15 ml) each.

Thick White Sauce: Follow recipe for Medium White Sauce, increasing butter and flour to 3 to 4 tablespoons (45 to 60 ml) each.

1 cup (250 ml)

Stuffed Peppers

These colorful beef and rice stuffed peppers are easy to prepare.

- 6 large green peppers, tops and seeds removed
- 1 1/2 teaspoons (7 ml) salt
- 1 pound (454 g) boneless beef chuck, cut in 1-inch (2.5 cm) pieces
- 1 small onion, quartered
- 1/2 cup (125 ml) uncooked quick-cooking rice
- 1/2 cup (125 ml) tomato sauce
- 1/2 teaspoon (2 ml) salt
- 1/4 teaspoon (1 ml) pepper
- 6 slices bacon

Put prepared green peppers into a large saucepan of boiling water with 1 1/2 teaspoons (7 ml) salt. Cover tightly and boil for 5 minutes. Drain, rinse with cold water, and put upside down on paper towels. Assemble Food Grinder with Fine Disc. Grind meat and onion into large bowl. Add remaining ingredients except bacon; mix well. Fill peppers with meat mixture and top each with a folded bacon slice. Set in 8×8×2-inch (20×20×5 cm) baking dish. Bake at 350°F (180°C) for 45 minutes. Serve hot.

6 servings

Ham Loaf with Horseradish Sauce

The garnish of pineapple adds flavor as well as color to complement the ham.

    2   pounds (907 g) boneless smoked ham,
          cut in 1-inch (2.5 cm) pieces
1 1/2   pounds (681 g) boneless pork,
          cut in 1-inch (2.5 cm) pieces
    1   medium onion, quartered
   18   soda crackers, broken
    2   eggs, slightly beaten
    1   cup (250 ml) hot milk
    1   can (8 ounces or 227 g) sliced
          pineapple, drained; reserve syrup
    1   teaspoon (5 ml) ground cinnamon
        Horseradish Sauce (below)

Assemble Food Grinder with Fine Disc. Grind ham, pork, onion, and soda crackers into bowl. Add eggs and milk; mix thoroughly. Shape into a loaf, score top, and set in a 13×9×2-inch (33×23×5 cm) baking pan. Mix pineapple syrup and cinnamon. Pour as much over loaf as will be absorbed. Bake at 350°F (180°C) for 1 hour; baste frequently with remaining syrup. Garnish with pineapple. Serve with Horseradish Sauce.

8 servings

Horseradish Sauce

Serve over meat such as ham loaf.

1/2   cup (125 ml) whipping cream
   1   tablespoon (15 ml) prepared
          horseradish
   1   teaspoon (5 ml) sugar
1/2   teaspoon (2 ml) lemon juice

Assemble Mixer. In small mixer bowl, whip cream at HIGH until stiff. Fold in remaining ingredients. Spoon into sauce bowl; chill.

1 cup (250 ml)

Barbecued Ribs

You'll need plenty of paper napkins when eating these crispy ribs.

    3   pounds (2.5 kg) pork loin back ribs
    1   cup (250 ml) chili sauce
1/2   cup (125 ml) ketchup
    6   tablespoons (90 ml) vinegar
1/2   cup (125 ml) honey
    2   tablespoons (30 ml) soy sauce
    1   tablespoon (15 ml) vegetable oil
    2   teaspoons (10 ml) Worcestershire
          sauce
    2   medium onions, quartered
    2   cloves garlic

Put pork ribs into a 13×9×2-inch (33×23×5 cm) baking pan. Assemble Blender. Put remaining ingredients into blender container. Cover and process 3 or 4 cycles at BLEND, or until onion is finely chopped. Pour over ribs. Bake at 325°F (160°C) for 1 1/2 hours. Cover pan with foil and bake an additional 30 minutes.

4 servings

Ham and Cheese Casserole

Prepare this easy casserole and a crisp green salad — your meal is ready to serve.

    1   cup (250 ml) milk
   10   soda crackers
1/2   pound (227 g) cooked ham, cut in
          1-inch (2.5 cm) pieces
1/2   pound (227 g) Swiss cheese,
          cut in 1-inch (2.5 cm) pieces
    5   eggs
    1   teaspoon (5 ml) Worcestershire Sauce

Warm milk in saucepan. Put crackers into milk; set aside. Assemble Food Grinder with Fine Disc. Grind ham and cheese into small mixer bowl. Assemble Mixer. In large mixer bowl, beat eggs at HIGH until light and thick (about 5 minutes). Add cracker mixture, ham-cheese mixture, and Worcestershire; fold with rubber spatula until evenly mixed. Pour into a greased 2-quart (2 liter) casserole. Bake at 350°F (180°C) for 30 minutes. Reduce temperature to 275°F (140°C) and bake an additional 30 minutes. Serve hot, plain or with Sweet Sour Mustard Sauce on page 109.

4 servings

Zucchini with Pork Stuffing

A ground meat, cheese, and onion mixture is blended with tomato sauce for an easy-to-prepare stuffing.

    1 large (2 pounds or 907 g) or 3 small
         (10 ounces or 280 g each) zucchini,
         halved and seeded
    1 pound (454 g) boneless pork shoulder,
         cut in 1-inch (2.5 cm) pieces
    1 medium onion, quartered
    6 ounces (170 g) Mozzarella
         cheese, cut in 1-inch
         (2.5 cm) pieces
    1 can (15 ounces or 425 g) tomato
         sauce with herbs
 1/2 cup (125 ml) water

Put zucchini halves into a greased 13×9×2-inch (33×23×5 cm) baking pan. Assemble Food Grinder with Fine Disc. Grind meat, onion, and cheese into large bowl. Add tomato sauce and mix thoroughly. Fill zucchini halves with pork mixture, mounding it high. Carefully pour water into bottom of pan; cover. Bake at 350°F (180°C) for 1 hour. Remove cover and bake an additional 30 minutes. Cut into portions or allow one half per serving.

6 servings

Sweet Sour Mustard Sauce

The perfect blend of sugar, mustard, and vinegar makes this sauce a fine companion for the Ham and Cheese Casserole.

 1/2 cup (125 ml) sugar
 1/2 teaspoon (2 ml) salt
    2 teaspoons (10 ml) dry mustard
    1 egg
 1/4 cup (50 ml) milk
 1/4 cup (50 ml) vinegar

Assemble Blender. Put all ingredients into blender container. Cover and process at LIQUEFY until blended. Pour into small saucepan and heat, stirring constantly, until sauce begins to thicken and boil. Serve warm.

1 cup (250 ml)

Polish Sausage

Pork is the meat used in this sausage.

         Sausage hog casings
    8 pounds (4 kg) boneless pork butt
         or pork shoulder, cut in 1-inch
         (2.5 cm) pieces
    2 tablespoons (30 ml) salt
    2 tablespoons (30 ml) mustard seed
 1 1/2 teaspoons (7 ml) crushed
         marjoram leaves
 1 1/2 teaspoons (7 ml) coarsely ground
         black pepper
    3 small cloves garlic, crushed with
         garlic press

Prepare sausage casing. Assemble Food Grinder with Fine Disc. Grind meat into large bowl. Combine seasonings and mix with meat. Reassemble food grinder with Medium Stuffing Tube. Stuff meat into casing. Twist or tie into desired number of links. Chill before separating links. Cook as desired.

8 pounds (4 kg)

Chop Suey

A hearty meal that is fun to prepare and serve to your special friends.

    2   tablespoons (30 ml) peanut oil
    3/4 pound (340 g) boneless lean pork
            shoulder, cut in 1/2-inch
            (1.3 cm) pieces
    3/4 pound (340 g) boneless veal shoulder,
            cut in 1/2-inch (1.3 cm) pieces
    1   cup (250 ml) beef broth
    2   large sweet onions, quartered
    3   large stalks celery, cut in 4-inch
            (10 cm) pieces
    1   can (8 ounces or 227 g) whole water
            chestnuts, drained
    1/4 cup (50 ml) soy sauce
    1/2 teaspoon (2 ml) bead molasses
    2   tablespoons (30 ml) cornstarch
    1   can (4 ounces or 114 g) mushroom
            pieces, drained
    1   can (16 ounces or 454 g) bean
            sprouts, drained
    1   can (8 ounces or 227 g) sliced
            bamboo shoots, drained
    4   cups (1 liter) cooked rice

Heat oil in a 5-quart (5 liter) Dutch oven or saucepan until hot. Add meat and brown quickly on all sides, stirring constantly. Add 1/2 cup (125 ml) beef broth; cover and simmer over medium-low heat for 20 minutes, or until meat is tender. Meanwhile, assemble Salad Maker with French Fry Cutter Disc and large bowl. Process onion. Change disc to Thick Slicer Disc and process celery and water chestnuts. Add processed vegetables to meat and stir to combine. Continue cooking covered for 15 minutes, or until celery and onion are crisp-tender. Mix soy sauce, remaining broth, molasses, and cornstarch. Pour into meat-vegetable mixture, add remaining vegetables, and stir well.

Bring to a boil, reduce heat, and simmer for 10 minutes. Serve with rice.

6 to 8 servings

Pork Sausage and Sauerkraut

Homemade sausage, sauerkraut, and noodles are layered for this crumb-topped casserole.

    1   pound (454 g) Country Pork Sausage
              (page 113)
    1 1/2 cups (375 ml) uncooked
              medium noodles
    1   can (16 ounces or 454 g)
              sauerkraut, drained
    1   tablespoon (15 ml) brown sugar
    1/2   teaspoon (2 ml) celery seed
    1   cup (250 ml) beef broth
    1   slice white bread, buttered

Shape sausage into 6 patties and brown in skillet on both sides. Remove patties; reserve 2 tablespoons (30 ml) drippings. Cook noodles in boiling, salted water as directed on package; drain. Mix noodles with reserved drippings. Spoon noodles into a greased 2-quart (2 liter) casserole. Mix sauerkraut with brown sugar and celery seed; spread over top of noodles. Put sausage patties on top. Pour beef broth over all. Set aside. Assemble Blender. Fold bread in half, buttered side in, and tear into 4 pieces. Put into blender container. Cover and process 2 cycles at GRATE to crumb bread. Sprinkle top of casserole with buttered crumbs. Bake at 350°F (180°C) for 30 to 40 minutes, or until crumbs are lightly browned.

3 or 4 servings

Ham Balls with Cherry Sauce

This cherry sauced ham ball recipe is quick to prepare.

Ham Balls:

- 2 slices white bread, torn in pieces
- 1 pound (454 g) cooked ham, cut in 1-inch (2.5 cm) pieces
- 1/2 pound (227 g) boneless veal, cut in 1-inch (2.5 cm) pieces
- 1/2 small onion
- 2 eggs, slightly beaten
- 2 tablespoons (30 ml) dried parsley flakes
- 2 tablespoons (30 ml) milk
- 1/4 teaspoon (1 ml) pepper
- 2 tablespoons (30 ml) vegetable oil

Cherry Sauce:

- 1 cup (25 ml) cherry jelly or preserves
- 2 tablespoons (30 ml) lemon juice
- 1 teaspoon (5 ml) ground cinnamon
- 1/4 teaspoon (1 ml) ground allspice

Assemble Food Grinder with Fine Disc. Grind bread, ham, veal, and onion into a bowl. Add eggs, parsley, milk, and pepper to bowl; mix well. Shape into walnut-size balls. Heat oil in large skillet. Add ham balls and brown on all sides over medium heat, then cook covered over low heat for 10 minutes. Meanwhile, for cherry sauce, mix all ingredients in small saucepan. Bring to a boil over low heat, stirring constantly. Put ham balls into warm shallow serving bowl and pour sauce over balls.

8 to 10 servings

Hong Kong Pork Chops

Serve with your choice of rice, mashed potatoes, or buttered noodles.

- 1 medium onion, halved
- 8 ounces (227 g) fresh mushrooms
- 1 can (5 ounces or 142 g) water chestnuts, drained
- 1/2 green pepper, seeded and halved
- 2 tablespoons (30 ml) vegetable oil
- 6 pork chops
- 1/4 cup (50 ml) orange juice
- 2 tablespoons (30 ml) lemon juice
- 1/4 cup (50 ml) soy sauce
- 1 clove garlic, mashed
- 1/2 teaspoon (2 ml) ginger
- 1 lemon, sliced

Assemble Salad Maker with Thick Slicer Disc and large bowl. Process onion, mushrooms and water chestnuts. Change disc to French Fry Cutter Disc and process green pepper. Set aside. Heat vegetable oil in skillet and brown chops on both sides. Put all remaining ingredients except sliced lemon into skillet. Simmer covered for 30 minutes, or until chops and vegetables are tender. Garnish with lemon slices.

6 servings

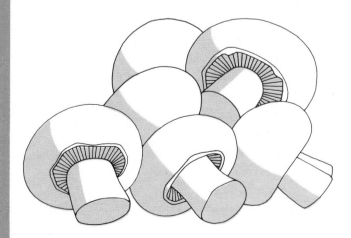

Italian Sausage and Eggplant

This meal-in-a-recipe has the influence of Italian cuisine.

    1   pound (454 g) Old-World Italian
         Sausage (page 116)
    1   small eggplant (about 1 pound
         or 454 g)
1 1/2   teaspoons (7 ml) salt
    2   medium green peppers, halved
         and seeded
    3   medium onions, quartered
    2   cloves garlic, mashed
  1/4   cup (50 ml) olive oil
    2   medium-size firm tomatoes, sliced
  1/4   cup (50 ml) chopped fresh parsley
    2   hot cherry peppers, quartered,
         cored, and seeded
    1   teaspoon (5 ml) oregano
    1   teaspoon (5 ml) rosemary, crushed
  1/2   teaspoon (2 ml) salt
         Dash pepper
    2   ounces (57 g) Parmesan cheese,
         cut in 1-inch (2.5 cm) cubes
         and chilled
  1/2   slice bread, torn in pieces
    4   cups (1 liter) cooked rice

Cut sausage into 1-inch (2.5 cm) pieces. Fry in skillet until lightly browned. Drain and set aside. Pare eggplant and cut into quarters lengthwise. Assemble Salad Maker with Chunky Cutter Disc. Process eggplant. Spread on paper towels, sprinkle with salt, and let drain 30 minutes. Change to French Fry Cutter Disc. Process green pepper, and onion; set aside. Heat 3 tablespoons (45 ml) olive oil in skillet, add green pepper, onion, and garlic; sauté, stirring occasionally, until vegetables are soft. Preheat oven to 375°F (190°C). Grease a 3-quart (3 liter) casserole. Put half of drained eggplant into bottom of casserole. Layer half of sausage, cooked vegetables, parsley, cherry pepper, and all of tomato slices.

Sprinkle with half of oregano, rosemary, salt, and pepper. Repeat layering and seasoning. Spoon remaining olive oil over top. Cover and bake at 375°F (190°C) for 30 minutes or until vegetables are tender. Meanwhile, assemble Blender. Cover blender container and set at BLEND. With motor on, remove feeder cap, and drop cheese cubes and bread pieces into container. Remove mixture and sprinkle over top of casserole. Bake uncovered at 350°F (180°C) for 10 minutes. Serve on cooked rice.

6 to 8 servings

Variation: Zucchini may be substituted for eggplant and cherry peppers omitted.

Country Pork Sausage

Shape seasoned meat into patties instead of links, if desired.

         Sausage hog casing
    8   pounds (4 kg) boneless pork butt
         or pork shoulder, cut in 1 1/2-inch
         (3.8 cm) pieces
    3   tablespoons (45 ml) salt
    2   teaspoons (10 ml) pepper
    2   teaspoons (10 ml) dried sage
  1/2   to 1 teaspoon (2 to 5 ml) ground
         red pepper or cayenne pepper

Prepare sausage casing. Assemble Food Grinder with Fine Disc. Grind meat into large bowl. Combine seasonings and mix with meat. Reassemble food grinder with Medium Stuffing Tube. Stuff meat into casing. Twist or tie into desired number of links. Chill thoroughly before separating links. Cook as desired.

8 pounds (4 kg)

Swedish Potato Sausage

Beef and pork are combined with potatoes and seasonings in this traditional Scandinavian sausage.

> Sausage hog casings
> 2 pounds (907 g) boneless beef chuck, cut in 1-inch (2.5 cm) cubes
> 2 pounds (907 g) boneless pork, cut in 1-inch (2.5 cm) cubes
> 2 pounds (907 g) potatoes, pared and cut in 1-inch (2.5 cm) cubes
> 3 medium onions, cut in 1 1/2- to 2-inch (3.8 to 5.0 cm) pieces
> 2 tablespoons (30 ml) salt
> 1 teaspoon (5 ml) ground allspice
> 1 teaspoon (5 ml) white pepper
> 1/2 cup (125 ml) water or ham stock

Prepare casing for stuffing. Assemble Food Grinder with desired Disc. Grind meat, potato, and onion into large bowl. Combine seasonings, add ingredients to bowl, and toss until well coated. Add 1/2 cup (125 ml) water gradually while stirring it into mixture. (If desired, shape into patties instead of preparing link sausages.) Reassemble Food Grinder with Coarse Disc and Medium Stuffing Tube. Stuff meat into casing. Twist or tie into desired number of links. Chill before separating links. If sausage is to be stored more than 2 or 3 days, it should be frozen. Cook using one of the following methods.

Panfried Method: Arrange sausage in cold skillet with 2 to 4 tablespoons (30 to 60 ml) water per pound. Cover and simmer 8 to 10 minutes over medium-low heat. Uncover and let water evaporate and sausage brown. Cook until well done.

Griddle or Skillet Method: Arrange sausage on cold griddle or in cold skillet. Cook over low heat, turning often, until well done (about 20 minutes).

6 1/2 pounds (3.0 kg)

Bratwurst

Sauerkraut is a fine accompaniment to bratwurst.

> Sausage hog casings
> 8 1/2 pounds (4.2 kg) pork and veal (We suggest about 6 pounds or 3 kg pork to about 2 1/2 pounds or 1.2 kg veal), cut in 1-inch (2.5 cm) cubes
> 2 1/2 tablespoons (37 ml) salt
> 5 teaspoons (25 ml) pepper
> 2 1/2 teaspoons (12 ml) ground nutmeg
> 2 1/2 teaspoons (12 ml) mace
> 1 teaspoon (5 ml) garlic salt
> 1 teaspoon (5 ml) mustard seed

Prepare casing for stuffing. Assemble Food Grinder with desired Disc. Grind meat into large bowl. Combine seasonings and mix with meat. Reassemble Food Grinder with Medium Stuffing Tube. Stuff meat into casing. Twist or tie into desired number of links. Chill thoroughly before separating links. Cook as desired.

8 1/2 pounds (4.2 kg)

Mustard Sauce

This sauce goes well with ham dishes.

> 1 teaspoon (5 ml) butter
> 1 teaspoon (5 ml) all-purpose flour
> 3/4 cup (200 ml) milk
> 2 egg yolks
> 1 tablespoon (15 ml) lemon juice
> 1 teaspoon (5 ml) dry mustard
> 1/4 teaspoon (1 ml) salt
> Dash white pepper

Assemble Blender. Put all ingredients into blender container. Cover and process at WHIP until well blended. Pour into saucepan and cook over low heat, stirring constantly until thick.

1 cup (250 ml)

Ravioli

A homemade treat that every family will be sure to enjoy.

> 3 to 3 1/2 cups (750 to 875 ml) all-purpose flour
> 2 eggs
> 1/2 cup (125 ml) water
> 1/2 teaspoon (2 ml) salt

Filling:

> 3/4 pound (340 g) boneless pork shoulder, cut in 1-inch (2.5 cm) cubes
> 1 small onion, quartered
> 1 package (10 ounces or 284 g) frozen chopped spinach, thawed and well drained
> 2 eggs, slightly beaten
> 1/2 cup (125 ml) blender grated Parmesan cheese
> 1/2 teaspoon (2 ml) salt
> 1/4 teaspoon (1 ml) pepper
> 1/8 teaspoon (0.5 ml) ground nutmeg
> 1 can (29 ounces or 822 g) tomato sauce
> 2 teaspoons (10 ml) dried Italian seasoning

Assemble Doughmaker. For pasta, in large mixer bowl, combine 2 cups (500 ml) flour, eggs, water, and salt. Knead with Doughmaker at recommended speed for about 3 minutes. Gradually add remaining flour to form stiff dough. Shape into a ball. Cover and let rest for 10 minutes. Assemble Food Grinder with Fine Disc. Grind pork and onion into small bowl. Heat large skillet and cook the meat and onion until meat is no longer pink; drain. Add spinach, eggs, cheese, salt, pepper, and nutmeg; stir well. Set aside. Stir tomato sauce and Italian seasoning together in saucepan and heat slowly over low heat, stirring occasionally.

To roll dough by hand: Divide dough into two portions. Working with one portion at a time on a lightly floured surface, roll dough very thin into 16×8-inch (40×20 cm) rectangle.

To make Ravioli: Working with one sheet of dough at a time, dip a pastry brush or index finger into a bowl of water and make vertical and horizontal lines in 2 1/2-inch (6.3 cm) squares. Put 1 tablespoon (15 ml) meat-spinach filling onto each square. Carefully spread a second sheet of rolled-out pasta on top of the first one, pressing down firmly around filling. With a ravioli cutter or sharp knife, cut pasta into squares as indicated, being sure all edges are sealed. Separate the mounds and set them on lightly floured waxed paper.

To cook and complete Ravioli: Fill a Dutch oven or saucepan (6 to 8 quarts or 6 to 8 liters) with water; add 2 teaspoons (10 ml) salt and 1 tablespoon (15 ml) olive oil. Bring to a rolling boil over high heat. Drop 12 ravioli at a time into the water; gently stir and cook 8 minutes, or until tender. Pour enough of the hot tomato sauce into a 13×9×2-inch (33×23×5 cm) baking pan to coat bottom of pan. Using a slotted spoon, carefully lift out cooked ravioli and arrange in pan. Cover with foil and keep hot until ready to serve. To prevent sticking, pour some hot sauce over ravioli in pan before adding more cooked ravioli.

32 ravioli

Old-World Italian Sausage

Prepare and serve as a main dish.

   Sausage hog casings
8 pounds (4 kg) boneless pork butt
   or pork shoulder, cut in 1-inch
   (2.5 cm) cubes
2 teaspoons (10 ml) salt
1 teaspoon (5 ml) black pepper
4 teaspoons (20 ml) fennel seed
4 teaspoons (20 ml) oregano leaves
1 teaspoon (5 ml) garlic powder
1 teaspoon (5 ml) ground red pepper
   or cayenne pepper (optional)

Prepare casing for stuffing. Assemble Food Grinder with desired Disc. Grind meat into large bowl. Combine seasonings and mix with meat. Reassemble Food Grinder with Medium Stuffing Tube. Stuff meat into casing. Twist or tie into desired number of links. Chill thoroughly before separating links. Cook as desired.

8 pounds (4 kg)

Veal Burger Steaks

Looking for something different for dinner? These vegetable-topped burgers have a crunchy taste appeal.

2 pounds (907 g) boneless veal, cut
   in 1-inch (2.5 cm) cubes
1 teaspoon (5 ml) salt
1/4 teaspoon (1 ml) pepper
1/4 teaspoon (1 ml) basil leaves
1 large onion, quartered
1 medium green pepper, quartered
   and seeded
10 fresh mushrooms
8 ounces (227 g) Mozzarella
   cheese, chilled

Assemble Food Grinder with Fine Disc. Grind meat into large bowl. Add salt and pepper; mix well. Set aside. Assemble Salad Maker with French Fry Cutter Disc and large bowl. Process onion, green pepper, and mushrooms. Set vegetables aside. Change disc to Shredder Disc. Process cheese; set aside. Shape meat into 8 patties and arrange on large broiler pan. Broil patties on one side until brown. Turn and broil for 3 minutes. Divide vegetables and cheese equally on patties. Broil until cheese is melted.

8 servings

Providential Veal au Gratin

An elegant main-dish casserole for those special dinners.

1 pound (454 g) boneless veal shoulder,
   cut in 1-inch (2.5 cm) pieces
1 clove garlic, mashed
1 teaspoon (5 ml) paprika
1/2 teaspoon (2 ml) thyme
1/4 cup (50 ml) butter, at
   room temperature
1 can (14 1/2 ounces or 411 g)
   asparagus spears, drained
2 cups (500 ml) unseasoned croutons
1 cup (250 ml) milk
2 tablespoons (30 ml) all-purpose
   flour
1 cup (250 ml) Cheddar cheese cubes
   (1-inch or 2.5 cm)
1/4 teaspoon (1 ml) salt
1/4 teaspoon (1 ml) pepper
1/2 cup (125 ml) slivered almonds

Toss veal pieces with garlic, paprika and thyme. Assemble Food Grinder with Fine Disc and small bowl. Grind seasoned veal. Shape veal into 4 patties. Melt 2 tablespoons (30 ml) butter in a large skillet over medium-high heat. Add patties and brown well on both sides. Cover skillet, reduce heat to medium-low, and cook until veal is done. Arrange asparagus spears in an 8×8×2-inch (20×20×5 cm) baking pan. Sprinkle with croutons. Top with the veal patties. Assemble Blender. Put remaining butter, milk, flour, cheese, salt, and pepper into blender container. Cover and process at CHOP until the cheese is finely chopped. Pour into a 2-quart (2 liter) saucepan and cook over medium-low heat, stirring constantly, until cheese is melted and sauce begins to thicken. Pour over veal and asparagus. Garnish patties with almonds. Bake at 350°F (180°C) for 30 minutes.

4 servings

Liver and Macaroni Casserole

Tomato sauce, liver cubes, and macaroni are layered in this tasty baked main dish.

 1 **pound (454 g) baby beef liver**
 3 **tablespoons (45 ml) butter or margarine**
 8 **ounces (227 g) Swiss cheese, cut in 1-inch (2.5 cm) cubes and chilled**
 1 **can (15 ounces or 425 g) tomato sauce with tomato bits**
 2 **tablespoons (30 ml) tomato paste**
 1 **medium onion, quartered**
 8 **fresh mushrooms**
 1 **teaspoon (5 ml) salt**
 1/8 **teaspoon (0.5 cm) crushed red pepper**
 1 **cup (250 ml) uncooked elbow macaroni, cooked and drained**

Heat butter in skillet and sauté liver over medium-low heat until all sides are brown. Drain, cut liver into 1/2-inch (1.3 cm) cubes, and set aside. Assemble Blender. Put 1 cup (250 ml) cheese into blender container. Cover and process 2 cycles at GRIND or until cheese is grated. Empty container and repeat with remain-

ing cheese. Set aside. Put remaining ingredients except liver and macaroni into blender container. Cover and process at GRATE until finely chopped. (If necessary, STOP BLENDER, use rubber spatula to keep ingredients around processing blades. Cover and continue to process.) Put macaroni into a greased 2-quart (2 liter) casserole. Spoon liver over macaroni. Pour sauce over all and sprinkle with cheese. Bake at 350°F (180°C) for 25 to 30 minutes.

6 to 8 servings

Western Eggs and Potatoes

This recipe joins fried eggs with shredded potato patties.

 3 **large potatoes, pared (see Note)**
 3 **tablespoons (45 ml) butter**
 Salt and pepper
 6 **eggs**
 Taco sauce

Assemble Salad Maker with Shredder Disc and large bowl. Process potatoes. Lightly butter a hot griddle or skillet. Form six (1/2-cup or 125 ml each) mounds of potatoes on griddle. Flatten with spoon and top each with 1 teaspoon (5 ml) butter. Cook for 5 to 7 minutes, or until browned. Turn potatoes with spatula and cook 5 minutes on other side. Sprinkle with salt and pepper. In separate skillet, fry 6 eggs in remaining butter. To serve, top each potato cake with fried egg. Pass taco sauce to season eggs.

6 servings

117

Chicken with Orange Sauce

Complement chicken with a tangy, spicy sauce.

- 1 **orange**
- 1 **green pepper, quartered and seeded**
- 2 **tablespoons (30 ml) soy sauce**
- 1/2 **cup (125 ml) chili sauce**
- 1 **teaspoon (5 ml) dry mustard**
- 1/2 **teaspoon (2 ml) garlic salt**
- 1 **tablespoon (15 ml) molasses**
- 1 **2 1/2-pound (1.2 kg) broiler-fryer chicken, quartered**

Assemble Citrus Juicer. Juice orange into glass measure (about 1/2 cup or 125 ml). Assemble Blender. Pour juice and remaining ingredients except chicken into blender container. Cover and process 2 or 3 cycles at CHOP, or until green pepper is finely chopped. Arrange chicken in a 9×9×2-inch (23×23×5 cm) baking pan. Pour sauce over the chicken. Bake at 350°F (180°C) for 45 minutes to 1 hour; baste occasionally. Serve hot.

4 servings

Chicken Loaf

Serve this loaf with a favorite sauce.

- 6 **slices bread, torn in quarters**
- 1 1/2 **cups chicken or turkey pieces (1-inch or 2.5 cm)**
- 1 **large onion, quartered**
- 1 **cup (250 ml) quick-cooking rice, uncooked**
- 1 **can (13 3/4 ounces or 390 g) chicken broth**
- 1 **teaspoon (5 ml) salt**
- 1/4 **teaspoon (1 ml) ground thyme**
- 4 **eggs**

Assemble Food Grinder with Coarse Disc. Grind bread, chicken, and onion into large bowl. Add remaining ingredients and stir well. Turn into a greased 9 1/4 × 5 1/4 × 2 3/4-inch (23 × 13 × 8 cm) loaf pan. Bake at 350°F (180°C) for 45 minutes.

4 to 6 servings

Apricot Stuffed Capon

Try preparing gravy from pan drippings.

- 8 **slices day-old bread, torn in pieces**
- 1/2 **cup (125 ml) dried apricots**
- 1/2 **cup (125 ml) walnuts**
- 2 **medium onions, quartered**
- 1 **stalk celery, cut in 1-inch (2.5 cm) pieces**
- 1 **clove garlic, minced**
- 1/2 **teaspoon (2 ml) salt**
- 1/2 **teaspoon (2 ml) poultry seasoning**
- 1/8 **teaspoon (0.5 ml) pepper**
- 1/2 **cup (125 ml) water**
- 1/4 **cup (50 ml) melted butter**
- 1 **fresh 6- to 7-pound (3 to 3.5 kg) capon, cleaned**
  Vegetable oil

Assemble Food Grinder with Coarse Disc. Grind bread, apricots, walnuts, onion, and celery into large bowl. Mix in garlic, dry seasonings, water, and butter. Stuff capon with dressing. Sew the opening together or fasten with skewers and lace with string. Tie around wings and legs to hold close to body. Put breast side up on rack in open roasting pan. Rub skin with a little vegetable oil. Roast at 325°F (160°C) for approximately 3 to 3 1/2 hours, or until done. To test for doneness: drumstick should move easily or meat thermometer should register 180° to 185°F (80° to 85°C) when inserted in thickest part of breast.

8 to 10 servings

Chicken in Rice

The blender makes this an easy-to-put-together meal.

    1 cup (250 ml) uncooked instant
         rice
    1 2 1/2-pound (1.3 kg) broiler-fryer
         chicken, quartered
    1 cup (250 ml) water
    1 can (10 3/4 ounces or 305 g)
         condensed cream of chicken soup
    1 can (8 ounces or 227 g) water
         chestnuts, drained
    1 medium onion, quartered
    1 stalk celery, cut in 1-inch
         (2.5 cm) pieces
  1/2 green pepper, seeded and cut
         in 1-inch (2.5 cm) pieces

Put rice into a 13 × 9 × 2-inch (33 × 23 × 5 cm) baking pan. Arrange chicken pieces over the rice. Assemble Blender. Put remaining ingredients into blender container. Cover and process 2 to 3 cycles at GRIND, or until vegetables are finely chopped. Pour over the chicken. Cover tightly with foil. Bake at 350°F (160°C) for 50 to 60 minutes.

4 servings

Cranberry Raisin Stuffing

This stuffing can be baked in a casserole for use as a side dish.

  1 1/2 cups (375 ml) fresh cranberries
      2 lemons, peeled (remove yellow
           portion only)
    3/4 cup (200 ml) sugar
    3/4 cup (200 ml) butter or
           margarine, melted
      2 cups (500 ml) seedless raisins,
           plumped
      2 teaspoons (10 ml) salt
      1 teaspoon (5 ml) ground cinnamon
      2 cups (500 ml) water or giblet
           broth
  2 1/2 quarts (2.5 liters) day-old
           white bread cut in 1-inch
           (2.5 cm) cubes

Assemble Food Grinder with Coarse Disc. Grind cranberries and lemon peel into small bowl. Stir in sugar, butter, raisins, salt, cinnamon, and water. Turn bread cubes into large bowl, add cranberry mixture, and toss until well mixed. Turn into a greased 4-quart (4 liter) casserole. Bake covered at 350°F (180°C) for 1 hour; stir gently after 30 minutes. Or use for poultry stuffing; roast as directed.

Enough for 16-pound (8 kg) turkey

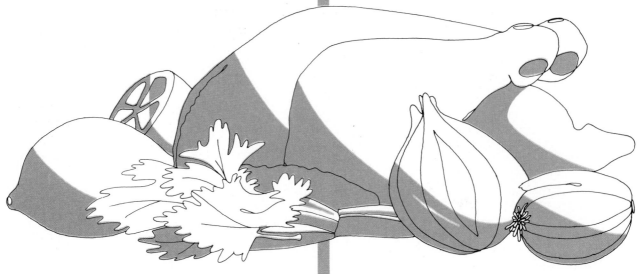

Crunchy Turkey Bake

A baked version of turkey à la king.

- 2 stalks celery, cut in 1-inch (2.5 cm) cubes
- 1 small onion, quartered
- 1/2 green pepper, seeded and quartered
- 4 ounces (113 g) fresh mushrooms
- 3 cups (750 ml) diced cooked turkey or chicken
- 1 jar (2 ounces or 57 g) sliced pimiento, drained
- 1 teaspoon (5 ml) poultry seasoning
- 1 can (10 3/4 ounces or 305 g) condensed cream of mushroom soup
- 1/3 cup (75 ml) milk
- 1 can (5 ounces or 142 g) chow mein noodles

Assemble Salad Maker with French Fry Cutter Disc and large bowl. Process celery, onion, and green pepper. Change disc to Thick Slicer Disc. Process mushrooms. Add turkey, pimiento, and poultry seasoning to bowl with vegetables; mix well. Put into a 2 1/2-quart (2.5 liter) casserole. Blend condensed soup and milk; pour over turkey mixture. Sprinkle chow mein noodles around edge of casserole. Bake at 350°F (180°C) for 50 minutes.

6 to 8 servings

Tartar Sauce

You will find that this sauce for fish is quickly prepared.

- 1/2 cup (125 ml) Blender Mayonnaise (page 97)
- 2 dill pickles, cut in 1-inch (2.5 cm) pieces
- 1 teaspoon (5 ml) lemon juice
- 1 slice onion
- 3 sprigs parsley, stems removed

Assemble Blender. Put all ingredients into blender container. Cover and process at BLEND until onion and pickles are chopped. Store in refrigerator.

3/4 cup (200 ml)

Tuna Casserole

Crisp rye rolls are a perfect accompaniment

- 4 slices bread
- 1/2 cup (125 ml) hot milk
- 8 ounces (227 g) sharp Cheddar cheese, cut in 1-inch (2.5 cm) cubes
- 1 green pepper, quartered and seeded
- 1 small onion, quartered
- 1 can (6 1/2 ounces or 184 g) tuna, drained
- 2 eggs
- 1 tablespoon (15 ml) lemon juice
- 1/4 teaspoon (1 ml) salt
- 1/8 teaspoon (0.5 ml) pepper

Assemble Grinder with Coarse Disc. Grind green pepper, onion, cheese, and bread into large bowl. Assemble Mixer. Combine all ingredients on LOW until well mixed. Put into 1-quart (1 liter) casserole. Bake at 350°F (180°C) for 45 minutes.

6 servings

Deep Sea Bake

Try this sauce with other varieties of fish.

- 1 **can (16 ounces or 454 g) whole tomatoes, drained**
- 1 **medium onion, quartered**
- 2 **bay leaves**
- 1/2 **teaspoon (2 ml) basil**
- 1/2 **teaspoon (2 ml) rosemary**
- 2 **tablespoons (30 ml) all-purpose flour**
- 1 **pound (454 g) frozen cod fillets, thawed**

Assemble Blender. Put drained tomatoes and remaining ingredients except fish into blender container. Cover and process at CHOP until vegetables and seasonings are finely chopped. Thoroughly rinse fish with cold water and pat dry. Put fish into a greased 1 1/2-quart (1.5 liter) flat-bottomed square casserole. Pour sauce over fish. Bake covered at 350°F (180°C) for 30 minutes, or until fish flakes easily when tested with a fork.

4 servings

Baked Trout with Apple Stuffing

This recipe is easy to cut in half for that special dinner for two.

- 3 **slices bread, halved**
- 1 **large tart apple, pared, cored, and quartered**
- 1/2 **teaspoon (2 ml) lemon juice**
- 1/2 **teaspoon (2 ml) sage**
- 1/4 **cup (50 ml) water**
- 4 **(6-ounce or 170 g each) whole rainbow trout**
- 3 **tablespoons (45 ml) butter**
- 3 **tablespoons (45 ml) lemon juice**

Assemble Salad Maker with Shredder Disc and large bowl. Process bread. Change disc to French Fry Cutter Disc and process apple into bowl with the bread. Stir in lemon juice, sage, and water. Carefully stuff each trout and put into a greased 13×9×2-inch (33×23×5 cm) baking pan. Heat butter and remaining lemon juice in small saucepan until butter is melted; pour over fish. Bake at 350°F (180°C) for 20 to 30 minutes, or until fish flakes when pierced with a fork. Serve with Tartar Sauce on page 121.

4 servings

Haddock in Herb Sauce

The subtle combination of seasonings gives this fish a unique flavor.

- 12 **ounces or (340 g) frozen haddock fillets, thawed**
- 1/2 **slice white bread**
- 1 **cup (250 ml) chicken broth**
- 1/4 **cup (50 ml) butter, at room temperature**
- 2 **tablespoons (30 ml) cornstarch**
- 1 **small onion, quartered**
- 2 **sprigs fresh parsley, stems removed, or 1 tablespoon (15 ml) dried parsley flakes**
- 1 **tablespoon (15 ml) ketchup**
- 1/2 **teaspoon (2 ml) salt**
- 1/2 **teaspoon (2 ml) prepared mustard**
- 1/4 **teaspoon (1 ml) chervil leaves**
- 1/4 **teaspoon (1 ml) marjoram leaves**
- 1/4 **teaspoon (1 ml) pepper**

Preheat oven to 350°F (180°C). Put fish into a greased 8×8×2-inch (20×20×5 cm) baking pan. Assemble Blender. Tear bread into 4 pieces. Put into blender container. Cover and process 2 cycles at GRATE to crumb bread. Set aside. Put remaining ingredients into blender container. Cover and process at CHOP until onion is finely chopped. Pour over fish and sprinkle with bread crumbs. Bake in preheated oven for 25 to 30 minutes, or until fish flakes easily when tested with a fork. Remove fish to serving plate. Stir sauce in pan until smooth. Pour over fish.

4 servings

Fettucini Pesto

With homemade noodles this is an extra-special treat to accompany your favorite meal.

Pasta:

    3 to 3 1/2 cups (750 to 875 ml)
         all-purpose flour
    2 eggs
    1/2 cup (125 ml) water
    1/2 teaspoon (2 ml) salt

Pesto:

    1 cup (250 ml) olive oil
    2 cups (500 ml) snipped parsley
    2 teaspoons (10 ml) basil leaves
    1 teaspoon (5 ml) salt
    1/4 teaspoon (1 ml) pepper
    1 clove garlic
    1/2 cup (125 ml) walnuts
    1/2 cup (125 ml) blender-grated
         Parmesan cheese

Assemble Doughmaker. For pasta, in large mixer bowl, combine 2 cups (500 ml) flour, eggs, water, and salt. Knead with doughmaker at recommended speed for about 3 minutes. Gradually add remaining flour to form a stiff dough. Shape into a ball. Cover and let rest for 10 minutes.

To roll dough by hand: Divide dough into two portions. Working with one portion at a time, roll out very thin. Cut with sharp knife into 1/8-inch (0.3 cm) strips. Let dry for 2 hours on floured cookie sheet or cook immediately.

To cook and complete Fettucini: Fill a Dutch oven or saucepan (6 to 8 quarts or 6 to 8 liters) with water; add 1 teaspoon (5 ml) salt and 1 teaspoon (5 ml) olive oil. Bring to a rolling boil over high heat. Shake off excess flour from pasta. Add to boiling water. Return to boil, stirring constantly. Cook pasta 3 to 5 minutes, or until al dente. Drain at once and rinse with hot water. Return to saucepan.

Assemble Blender. Put ingredients for Pesto into blender container. Cover and process at LIQUEFY until mixture is smooth. Pour over hot cooked fettucini and toss.

8 to 10 servings

Spaghetti and Meatballs

This spicy Italian dinner will satisfy hearty appetites.

    1 can (29 ounces or 822 g)
         tomato sauce
    1 can (12 ounces or 340 g)
         tomato paste
    1 cup (250 ml) water
    1 medium onion, halved
    1/2 green pepper, seeded
    10 fresh mushrooms
    1/2 teaspoon (2 ml) garlic powder
    2 bay leaves
    1/2 teaspoon (2 ml) basil leaves
    1/2 teaspoon (2 ml) marjoram leaves
    1/4 teaspoon (1 ml) ground thyme
    1 tablespoon (15 ml) dry vermouth
         Italian Meatballs (page 102)
    3/4 to 1 pound (340 to 454 g)
         spaghetti, cooked

Put tomato sauce, tomato paste, and water into 5-quart (5 liter) Dutch oven or saucepot. Stir to mix. Assemble Salad Maker with French Fry Cutter Disc and small bowl. Process onion and green pepper. Change disc to Thick Slicer Disc and carefully slice mushrooms. Add vegetables and remaining ingredients except meatballs to tomato sauce; stir. Bring to a boil over medium-high heat, reduce heat to low, and simmer for 45 minutes, stirring as necessary. Add meatballs to sauce and simmer for 1 hour. Serve hot over spaghetti.

6 to 8 servings

Pick Your Own

Side dishes can steal the show when they're as tempting as Mixed Vegetable Casserole, Danish Sweet and Sour Cabbage, and Baked Carrots Supreme. The bright colors and crisp textures of Vegetable Stir-Fry, Marinated Carrots, and Zucchini Pancakes will no doubt command second helpings.

But what you must be prepared for, above all, with the Oster "Kitchen Center" appliance is this: You and your family will fall in love with potatoes! It is so easy to make French Fries, Whipped Potatoes, and Potato Pancakes that you can feast on these favorites every night. For added convenience, you can follow the recipes for Do-Ahead Fries, Freeze Your Own Fries, or Oven-Baked French Fries. No potato-peeling is required! And when you're ready for a change-of-pace or a holiday dinner, you can switch your spud specialty to Potato Cheese Casserole, elegant Duchess Potatoes, or Double Baked Sweet Potatoes.

Mixed Vegetable Casserole

The natural taste of these vegetables makes this an appealing dish.

  1 **small yellow summer squash, halved**
  1 **small zucchini, halved**
  1 **medium onion, halved**
  1 **medium green pepper, halved**
    and seeded
  1 **large tomato, sliced and quartered**
  1 **teaspoon (5 ml) dried**
    Italian seasoning
1/2 **teaspoon (2 ml) salt**
  1 **tablespoon (15 ml) oil**

Assemble Salad Maker with Thick Slicer Disc and large bowl. Process each vegetable except tomato. Heat oil in fry pan over medium heat. Saute all vegetables except tomatoes until crisp tender. Add tomatoes and cook until heated through.

4 servings

Carrot Ring

An all-time favorite that gives the sweet flavor of carrots a lift.

- 2 **tablespoons (30 ml) corn flake crumbs**
- 4 **large carrots**
- 3/4 **cup (200 ml) butter or margarine, at room temperature**
- 1/3 **cup (75 ml) firmly packed brown sugar**
- 2 **eggs**
- 1 **tablespoon (15 ml) lemon juice**
- 1 1/2 **cups (375 ml) all-purpose flour**
- 1 **teaspoon (5 ml) baking powder**
- 1 **teaspoon (5 ml) baking soda**
- 1/2 **teaspoon (2 ml) salt**

Generously grease a 1 1/4-quart (1.25 liter) glass ring mold. Sprinkle crumbs over sides and bottom, tipping and patting to coat evenly; set aside. Assemble Salad Maker with Shredder Disc and large bowl. Process carrots (about 1 quart or 1 liter). Set aside. Assemble Mixer. In large mixer bowl, mix remaining ingredients at MEDIUM-LOW until well mixed, adding carrots near the end. Spread evenly in mold. Bake at 350°F (180°C) for 40 minutes. Let stand for 5 minutes. Unmold and cut into slices. If desired, fill center with a colorful vegetable.

6 servings

Baked Carrots Supreme

When you combine basil and carrots, you have a delicious combination.

- 1 **pound (454 g) carrots, pared**
- 1 **small onion, halved**
- 1/4 **cup (50 ml) water**
- 2 **tablespoons (30 ml) butter**
- 1 1/2 **teaspoons (7 ml) salt**
- 1/4 **teaspoon (1 ml) basil leaves**

Assemble Salad Maker with Shredder Disc. Process carrots into a buttered 1-quart (1 liter) casserole. Change disc to French Fry Cutter Disc and process onion; mix well. Put water, butter, salt, and basil into small saucepan; heat until butter is melted and pour over carrot mixture. Cover casserole. Bake at 375°F (190°C) for 50 to 55 minutes, or until vegetables are tender.

6 servings

Marinated Carrots

This may be served as a cold vegetable for a summer day or as a salad.

- 2 **pounds (907 g) fresh carrots, pared**
- 1 **medium onion, quartered**
- 1 **green pepper, quartered and seeded**
- 2 **stalks celery, cut in 4-inch (10 cm) lengths**
- 1 **can (10 3/4 ounces or 305 g) condensed tomato soup**
- 1/2 **cup (125 ml) sugar**
- 1/2 **cup (125 ml) vinegar**
- 1/2 **cup (125 ml) vegetable oil**
- 1/4 **cup (50 ml) snipped parsley**

Assemble Salad Maker with Thick Slicer Disc. Process carrots into a 3-quart (3 liter) saucepan. Parboil carrots in salted water until crisp-tender; drain and keep hot. Change disc to French Fry Cutter Disc. Process onion, green pepper and celery; set aside. Assemble Blender. Put condensed tomato soup, sugar, vinegar, and oil into blender container. Cover and process at CHOP until well blended. Pour into saucepan and add green pepper, celery, and onion. Bring to a boil. Turn hot carrots into a bowl and pour hot sauce over carrots; cover tightly and chill overnight or longer. Store no longer than a week in refrigerator. When ready to serve, garnish with parsley.

10 to 12 servings

Vegetable Stir-Fry

A colorful combination of vegetables to serve with your choice of meat, fish, or poultry.

    2   small carrots, pared
    2   stalks celery, cut in 4-inch
            (10 cm) lengths
    1   can (8 ounces or 227 g) water
            chestnuts, drained
    1   small zucchini
    1   small onion, halved
  1/2   green pepper, seeded
    3   tablespoons (45 ml) vegetable oil
    1   teaspoon (5 ml) cornstarch
  1/2   cup (125 ml) chicken broth
        Dash pepper
   12   cherry tomatoes

Assemble Salad Maker with Thin Slicer Disc and large bowl. Process carrots. Change disc to Thick Slicer Disc and process celery and water chestnuts. Change disc to French Fry Cutter Disc and process zucchini, onion, and green pepper. Heat oil in a skillet and stir-fry all vegetables except tomatoes until crisp-tender. Dissolve cornstarch in broth. Add to skillet and stir constantly until it starts to thicken. Add pepper and tomatoes; stir carefully just until heated and well mixed.

6 servings

Curried Cabbage

This is a quickly prepared vegetable to serve with roast meat or poultry.

    1   medium head (about 2 pounds or
            907 g) cabbage, cut in wedges
    2   tablespoons (30 ml) butter
  1/2   teaspoon (2 ml) salt
  1/2   to 1 teaspoon (2 to 5 ml)
            curry powder

Assemble Salad Maker with Thin Slicer Disc and large bowl. Process cabbage Melt butter in skillet; add salt, curry powder, and cabbage. Cover and simmer about 10 minutes; stir occasionally.

4 servings

Layered Vegetable Casserole

A cheesy, colorful vegetable combination.

    1   cup (250 ml) Cheddar cheese cubes
            (1 inch or 2.5 cm), chilled
    2   carrots, pared
  1/2   pound (227 g) fresh green beans,
            rinsed and ends removed
  1/2   green pepper, seeded and halved
  1/2   small head cauliflower, broken
            in flowerets
    1   cup (250 ml) broccoli flowerets
  1/2   cup (125 ml) Italian salad dressing

Assemble Blender. Cover blender container and set at BLEND. With motor on, remove feeder cap, and drop cheese cubes into container. Assemble Salad Maker with Thin Slicer Disc. Slice carrots and put into a 2-quart (2 liter) casserole. Top carrots with 1/3 cup (75 ml) grated cheese. Change disc to Thick Slicer Disc. Cut beans so they will fit horizontally in hopper. Process and put on top of cheese in casserole. Change disc to French Fry Cutter Disc. Process green pepper and cauliflower; put on top of beans. Sprinkle with remaining cheese. Top with broccoli. Pour dressing over casserole. Bake covered at 350°F (180°C) for 45 minutes, or until vegetables are tender.

6 to 8 servings

Potato Cheese Casserole

A cheese soup sauce and potato bake.

- 3 or 4 large potatoes, pared and quartered
- 1 can (11 ounces or 312 g) condensed Cheddar cheese soup
- 1/2 cup (125 ml) milk
- 1/2 teaspoon (2 ml) salt
- 1 tablespoon (15 ml) butter or margarine, at room temperature
- 1 tablespoon (15 ml) snipped parsley

Assemble Salad Maker with Shredder Disc and large bowl. Process potatoes; you should have 4 cups (1 liter) shredded potatoes. Add remaining ingredients except parsley and mix well. Pour into a buttered 1 1/2-quart (1.5 liter) casserole. Sprinkle parsley over top. Bake uncovered in a preheated 350°F (180°C) oven for 1 hour, or until potatoes are tender.

6 servings

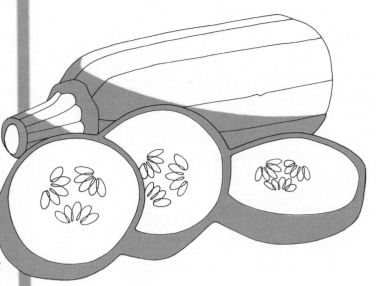

Cheesy Zucchini Casserole

An unusual trio of vegetables with butter sauce is baked together.

- 3 medium zucchini
- 1 medium onion, halved
- 1/2 green pepper, seeded and halved
- 6 tablespoons (90 ml) butter
- 1/4 cup (50 ml) all-purpose flour
- 1/2 teaspoon (2 ml) salt
- 1/4 teaspoon (1 ml) pepper
- 6 ounces (170 g) Mozzarella cheese

Assemble Salad Maker with Thick Slicer Disc and large mixer bowl. Slice zucchini, place in 1 1/2 quart (1.5 liter) casserole. Slice onion and green pepper, sauté in 2 tablespoons (30 ml) butter until tender. Put into casserole. Melt remaining butter in small saucepan. Remove from heat and stir in flour, salt, and pepper. Pour over vegetables. Change disc to Shredder Disc. Process cheese (about 1 1/2 cups or 375 ml). Sprinkle cheese over vegetables. Cover casserole. Bake at 350°F (180°C) for 35 to 40 minutes. Serve hot.

6 to 8 servings

Danish Sweet and Sour Cabbage

Cooking the red cabbage in sweet-sour sauce results in an appealing wine-colored vegetable.

> 1 **medium head (about 2 pounds or 907 g) red cabbage, cut in wedges**
> 1/4 **cup (50 ml) butter or margarine**
> 1/2 **cup (125 ml) water**
> 1/3 **cup (75 ml) vinegar**
> 1/3 **cup (75 ml) red currant jelly**
> 1 **teaspoon (5 ml) salt**
> 1/2 **teaspoon (2 ml) caraway seed or celery seed**

Assemble Salad Maker with Thick Slicer Disc. Process cabbage (about 1 1/2 quarts or 1.5 liters) into 4-quart (4 liter) saucepan. Add remaining ingredients and stir. Bring to a boil over medium heat, reduce heat, and simmer covered for 1 1/2 hours, stirring occasionally; if cabbage looks dry, add a little more water.

6 servings

Orange Glazed Beets

The citrus glaze turns beets into a vegetable delight.

> 2 **pounds (907 g) fresh beets, cooked and peeled**
> 1 **orange**
> 1 **lemon**
> 2 **tablespoons (30 ml) butter, at room temperature**
> 2 **tablespoons (30 ml) sugar**
> 1 **tablespoon (15 ml) cornstarch**
> 1/2 **teaspoon (2 ml) salt**
> 1 **tablespoon (15 ml) vinegar**

Assemble Salad Maker with Thick Slicer Disc. Process beets into medium saucepan; set aside. Assemble Citrus Juicer. Juice orange and lemon into glass measure (about 1/2 cup or 125 ml orange juice and 1/4 cup or 50 ml lemon juice). Assemble Blender. Pour juice into blender container and add remaining ingredients. Cover and process at BLEND until well mixed. Pour over beets in saucepan and cook until hot and thickened, stirring as necessary.

6 to 8 servings

Oven-Baked French Fries

Serve these fries as you would regular French Fries.

> 4 **cups (1 liter) potatoes cut for French Fries (page 133)**
> 1/4 **cup (50 ml) melted butter or margarine**
> **Seasoned salt to taste**

Blot raw potatoes dry with paper towels. Arrange potatoes in a 13×9×2-inch (33×22×5 cm) baking pan and drizzle with melted butter. Bake at 450°F (230°C) for 35 to 40 minutes, or until golden brown. Stir potatoes several times during the baking period. Remove to paper towels to drain. Sprinkle with seasoned salt.

4 servings

Whipped Potatoes

These basic whipped potatoes need only a topping of gravy or butter, if desired.

> 6 medium potatoes, pared and quartered
> 1 quart (1 liter) boiling water
> 1 teaspoon (5 ml) salt
> 1/3 cup (75 ml) milk or cream
> 3 tablespoons (45 ml) butter, at
>   room temperature

Boil potatoes in water with 1/2 teaspoon (2 ml) salt about 20 minutes, or until tender. Drain well; reserve stock for soup base or bread, if desired. Assemble Mixer. In large mixer bowl, mix potatoes, milk, butter, and 1/2 teaspoon (2 ml) salt at MEDIUM until creamy.

4 to 6 servings

French Fries

An easy way to prepare potatoes.

> Potatoes
> Vegetable oil for frying
> Salt to taste

Heat oil to 400°F (200°C) in a deep fryer. Assemble Salad Maker with French Fry Cutter Disc and large bowl. Process desired amount of potatoes. Blot any starch or water from potatoes with paper towel to avoid excess spattering while frying. Put recommended amount of raw potatoes into basket. Lower basket carefully into hot oil and cook until golden brown. Raise fries from oil, let oil drain off, and put potatoes on paper towels to complete draining. Salt and serve immediately. Repeat as necessary.

Shoestring Potatoes: Follow recipe for French Fries using Shredder Disc to process potatoes.

Do-Ahead Fries

French Fries can be precooked early in the day and fried crisp and golden later.

French Fries (page 133)

Prepare potatoes as directed and fry in 400°F (200°C) oil for 1 minute. Remove and let drain on paper towels. Cover and refrigerate until serving time. To finish, fry potatoes for 1 to 2 minutes in 400°F (200°C) oil. Drain well, salt, and serve.

Double Baked Sweet Potatoes

Peanut butter is the surprise ingredient in the stuffing.

> 6 medium sweet potatoes
> 1/2 cup (125 ml) milk
> 3 tablespoons (45 ml) butter or
>   margarine, at room temperature
> 1/2 cup (125 ml) Blender Peanut Butter
>   (page 48)
> 1 teaspoon (5 ml) salt
> 1/2 teaspoon (2 ml) ground allspice
>   Dash pepper

Preheat oven to 425°F (220°C). Scrub potatoes, dry on paper towels, and put on a cookie sheet. Bake for 1 hour, or until soft when pricked with fork. Cut slice lengthwise from top of each potato; scoop out insides, being careful not to break shell. Put potato pulp into large mixer bowl. Assemble Mixer. Add milk, butter, peanut butter, salt, and allspice to potato pulp. Mix at MEDIUM until potato mixture is smooth and fluffy. Add more milk if necessary. Spoon into shells. Bake for 15 to 20 minutes, or until tops are lightly browned.

6 servings

Duchess Potatoes

This purée may be used as a garnish or as a main dish accompaniment.

- 4 medium potatoes
- 2 stalks celery
- 1 medium onion
- 1 tablespoon (15 ml) butter, melted
- 1 egg, slightly beaten
- 1/4 teaspoon (1 ml) salt
  Dash pepper

Cook potatoes, celery, and onion covered in large saucepan with water until tender. Drain well. Preheat oven to 400°F (200°C). Assemble "Power Purée 'N Ricer" accessory. Process potatoes, celery, and onion at HIGH into large bowl. Add remaining ingredients and mix well. Drop by tablespoonfuls or form rosettes with pastry bag onto greased cookie sheet. Bake in preheated oven for 15 minutes, or until lightly browned.

5 or 6 servings

Zucchini Pancakes

Serve these crisp, cheesy pancakes as a vegetable side dish or as the main course of a light meal.

- 1 medium zucchini
- 1 cup (250 ml) Cheddar cheese cubes (1-inch or 2.5 cm), chilled
- 2 eggs
- 1/2 cup (125 ml) milk
- 2/3 cup (200 ml) biscuit mix
- 1/4 cup (50 ml) wheat germ
- 1/4 cup (50 ml) grated Parmesan cheese
- 1/4 teaspoon (1 ml) pepper

Assemble Salad Maker with Shredder Disc and large mixer bowl. Shred zucchini. Assemble Blender. Cover blender container and set at BLEND. With motor on, remove feeder cap and drop cheese cubes into container. Put in bowl with zucchini. Put remaining ingredients into blender container in order listed. Cover and process at MIX until well combined. Pour over zucchini and cheese; mix with a spoon. Ladle onto a buttered hot griddle over medium heat; cook, browning both sides. Serve with butter, salt, and pepper.

6 to 8 servings

Potato Pancakes

Serve as a meat accompaniment.

- 2 eggs
- 1 small onion, quartered
- 2 tablespoons (30 ml) all-purpose flour
- 1 teaspoon (5 ml) salt
- 1/4 teaspoon (1 ml) baking powder
- 3 cups (750 ml) raw potato cubes

Assemble Blender. Put eggs, onion, flour, salt, baking powder, and 1/2 cup (125 ml) potato cubes into blender container. Cover and process at GRATE until smooth. Add remaining potatoes, cover, and process 2 cycles at GRIND. Pour onto well-greased hot griddle; over medium heat cook, browning both sides. Drain on absorbent paper, if necessary.

12 pancakes

Freeze Your Own Fries

The precooked fries will remain loose in the freezer bag, so that any amount can easily be removed.

French Fries (page 133)

Prepare potatoes as directed and fry in 400°F (200°C) oil for 1 minute. Drain well on paper towels. Place in one layer on baking sheet. Freeze until solid. Pack fries in freezer bags and store until ready to use. When ready to fry, remove desired amount of fries from freezer. Fry in 400°F (200°C) oil for 1 to 2 minutes, or until golden brown. Drain well, salt, and serve.

Celery Amandine

This unusual side dish is sure to become a family favorite.

     1 **bunch celery, thick sliced,**
        top leaves reserved
   1/4 **cup (50 ml) butter or margarine**
   1/4 **cup (50 ml) flour**
     1 **teaspoon (5 ml) salt**
     1 **cup (250 ml) milk**
   1/2 **cup (125 ml) celery water**
   1/3 **cup (50 ml) almonds or walnuts**

Preheat oven to 350°F (180°C). Cook celery in 1-quart (1 liter) of boiling water for 10 to 12 minutes. Drain, reserve 1/2 cup (125 ml) cooking water. Assemble Blender. Put milk, butter, salt and flour into blender container. Cover and process at WHIP. Add celery tops and process 1 cycle at CHOP. Pour into saucepan and add reserved celery water. Heat until thick, stirring constantly. Put half of celery into a buttered 1-quart (1 liter) casserole. Pour over half the sauce. Repeat. Put

almonds in "Mini-Blend" container and process 2 cycles at GRIND. Sprinkle over the top of casserole. Bake uncovered 30 minutes.

6 servings

Egg Foo Yung

Eggs and vegetables combine in this time-honored Oriental favorite.

     6 **eggs**
     1 **can (6 ounces or 170 g) water**
        chestnuts, drained
   1/2 **green pepper, cut into 1-inch**
        (2.5 cm) pieces
   1/2 **teaspoon (2 ml) salt**
     1 **medium onion, cut in eighths**
     1 **package (10 ounces or 284 g)**
        frozen spinach, cooked and
        drained or 1 can (15 ounces
        or 426 g) chopped spinach,
        well drained

Assemble Blender. Put all ingredients except spinach in blender container. Cover and process at CHOP 3 to 4 cycles. Pour into mixing bowl, add spinach, and stir to mix well. Pour mixture by tablespoonfuls onto hot griddle and bake until brown on medium heat. Turn and brown other side. Serve with Oriental Sauce.

Oriental Sauce
   3/4 **cup (200 ml) water**
     1 **tablespoon (15 ml) cornstarch**
     2 **tablespoons (30 ml) soy sauce**
     1 **tablespoon (15 ml) sugar**
     1 **tablespoon (15 ml) cider**
        vinegar

Combine all ingredients and cook in 1-quart (1 liter) saucepan over medium heat until clear and thickened.

4 to 6 servings

The Bake Shop

If you'd just as soon begin meals with dessert, start baking these confections right away! Chocolate lovers will head straight for the moist, scrumptious Chocolate Quick Cake or the Frosted Chocolate Cake Bars. Those who can't resist fruit flavors will have a hard time choosing among Apple Carrot Cake, Banana Brownies, and Holiday Orange Cake. And cookie-lovers will quickly polish off batches of Peanut Butter Oatmeal Cookies, Brown Sugar Crisps, and Mom's Molasses Cookies.

If homemade pies are your absolute favorite, you'll be delighted by the easy recipe for flaky pastry — just be sure not to overmix the dough. Crumb crusts of all kinds are just as simple and virtually instant, since they don't require rolling. No-bake desserts include a wonderfully rich Strawberry Ice Cream made with the juice extracted from whole berries. And calorie-counters needn't feel deprived — the flavors of Fresh Applesauce and Heavenly Angel Food Cake are yours to savor.

Hawaiian Fruit Cake

A quickly mixed cake that has butter in the frosting only.

- 1 cup (250 ml) walnuts
- 2 cups (500 ml) all-purpose flour
- 2 cups (500 ml) sugar
- 1 teaspoon (5 ml) baking soda
- 2 eggs
- 1 can (20 ounces or 566 g) crushed pineapple

Preheat oven to 350°F (180°C). Assemble Blender. Put walnuts into blender container. Cover and process 2 cycles at WHIP to chop nuts; set aside. Assemble Mixer. In large mixer bowl, mix flour, sugar, baking soda, eggs, pineapple with syrup, and nuts at MEDIUM-LOW until mixed. Pour into a greased 13×9×2-inch (33×23×5 cm) baking pan. Bake in preheated oven 40 minutes, or until toothpick inserted in center comes out clean. Cool in pan on rack. Frost with Butter Cream Cheese Frosting (page 143).

18 servings

Greek Cake

The flavor of citrus permeates this moist party cake.

Cake:

- 4 **eggs**
- 3/4 **cup (200 ml) sugar**
- 1/4 **pound (113 g) butter, at room temperature**
- 1/2 **teaspoon (2 ml) vanilla extract**
  Grated peel of 1/2 orange
- 1 **cup (250 ml) all-purpose flour**
- 1 1/2 **teaspoons (7 ml) baking powder**
- 1/4 **teaspoon (1 ml) salt**
- 2 **tablespoons (30 ml) farina**

Syrup:

- 1 **orange**
- 1 **lemon**
- 1 **cup (250 ml) sugar**
- 1 **cup (250 ml) water**
  Whipped Cream
  Orange Slices

For Cake, preheat oven to 350°F (180°C). Assemble Mixer. Separate eggs, putting whites into small mixer bowl and yolks into large mixer bowl. Beat whites at MEDIUM-HIGH until frothy, then add 1/2 cup (125 ml) sugar gradually while beating until stiff peaks form. Set aside. Add butter, remaining sugar, vanilla extract, grated peel, and dry ingredients to yolks and beat at LOW until flour is moistened then at MEDIUM-HIGH until smooth. Gently stir beaten whites into yolk mixture. Pour into a well-greased 9×9×2-inch (23×23×5 cm) baking pan. Bake in preheated oven for 50 to 55 minutes, or until top springs back when touched with finger. While cake is baking, prepare Syrup. For Syrup, assemble Citrus Juicer. Juice orange and lemon into 1-quart (1 liter) saucepan; use 1/2 cup (125 ml) juice. Add sugar and water. Bring to boil, stirring constantly until sugar is dissolved; boil for 5 minutes. Pour syrup carefully over hot cake; cool several hours to absorb syrup. Cut into diamonds. Serve topped with whipped cream and orange slices.

16 squares

Apple Carrot Cake

Cream Cheese Glaze is the suggested icing for this raisin spice cake.

- 4 **large tart apples, pared, cored, and quartered**
- 4 **carrots, pared**
- 3 **cups (750 ml) all-purpose flour**
- 1 **tablespoon (15 ml) baking soda**
- 1/2 **teaspoon (2 ml) salt**
- 1 **tablespoon (15 ml) ground cinnamon**
- 1 **teaspoon (5 ml) ground nutmeg**
- 4 **eggs**
- 3/4 **cup (200 ml) vegetable oil**
- 2 **cups (500 ml) sugar**
- 1 **teaspoon (5 ml) vanilla extract**
- 1 **cup (250 ml) raisins**

Preheat oven to 350°F (180°C). Assemble Salad Maker with Shredder Disc and large bowl. Process apples and carrots; set aside. Assemble Mixer. In large mixer bowl, beat remaining ingredients at LOW until dry ingredients are blended then at MEDIUM until smooth. Add apple-carrot mixture and mix well at LOW. Pour into greased 13×9×2-inch (33×23×5 cm) baking pan. Bake in preheated oven for 50 to 55 minutes or until toothpick inserted near center comes out clean. Cool thoroughly before frosting with Cream Cheese Glaze on page 148.

16 servings

Lemon-Lime Soda Cake

The lemon-lime soda makes this version of pound cake light and airy.

1 1/2	**cups (375 ml) butter, or margarine at room temperature**
3	**cups (750 ml) sugar**
5	**eggs**
3	**cups (750 ml) all-purpose flour**
1	**teaspoon (5 ml) almond extract**
3/4	**cup (200 ml) lemon-lime soda**

Preheat oven to 325°F (160°C). Assemble Mixer. In large mixer bowl, cream butter and sugar at LOW. Add eggs, one at a time, while continuing to mix at LOW. Add flour, almond extract, and lemon-lime soda; mix at LOW then at MEDIUM-LOW until well blended. Pour batter into greased 14-cup (3.5 liter) fluted tube pan. Bake in preheated oven for 1 hour and 15 minutes, or until toothpick inserted near center comes out clean. Cool 15 minutes. Remove from pan and sprinkle generously with confectioners sugar or serve with Cherry Dessert Sauce on page 147.

16 servings

Buttery Loaf Cake

This buttery loaf cake is a traditional favorite.

1	**pound (454 g) butter, at room temperature**
2 1/2	**cups (625 ml) confectioners sugar**
1	**tablespoon (15 ml) vanilla extract**
6	**eggs**
3	**cups (750 ml) all-purpose flour**

Preheat oven to 325°F (160°C). Assemble Mixer. In large mixer bowl, cream butter, sugar, and vanilla extract at MEDIUM-LOW. While mixing, add eggs one a time. Add flour and slowly increase to HIGH until blended. Divide batter between 2 well-greased 8 1/2×4 1/2×2 5/8-inch (22×11×7 cm) loaf pans. Cut through batter with a rubber spatula. Bake in preheated oven for 1 hour and 15 minutes, or until toothpick inserted near center comes out clean. Let cool completely before removing from pan. Serve plain or with Velvety Lemon Sauce on page 147.

2 loaf cakes

Note: If desired, wrap cooled cake securely and store in freezer.

Chocolate Quick Cake

The canned chocolate syrup helps to make this an easily prepared and moist cake.

1	**cup (250 ml) all-purpose flour**
1	**cup (250 ml) sugar**
1	**teaspoon (5 ml) baking powder**
1/2	**cup (125 ml) butter or margarine, at room temperature**
1	**can (16 ounces or 454 g) chocolate syrup**
1	**teaspoon (5 ml) vanilla extract**
4	**eggs**

Preheat oven to 350°F (180°C). Asssemble Mixer. In large mixer bowl, mix all ingredients at LOW until dry ingredients are moistened then at MEDIUM until smooth. Pour batter into 2 well-greased 8-inch (20 cm) round layer cake pans or one 13×9×2-inch (33×23×5 cm) baking pan. Bake in preheated oven for 25 minutes for layers and 30 minutes for large cake or until toothpick inserted near center comes out clean. When cool, frost with desired frosting.

12 to 16 servings

Zucchini Chocolate Cake

No frosting is needed on this moist spice cake.

           2 medium zucchini
       1/2 cup (125 ml) butter or margarine,
                at room temperature
       1/2 cup (125 ml) vegetable oil
   1 3/4 cups (450 ml) sugar
           2 eggs
           1 teaspoon (5 ml) vanilla extract
       1/2 cup (125 ml) dairy sour cream
                or yogurt
   2 1/2 cups (625 ml) all-purpose flour
           1 teaspoon (5 ml) baking soda
       1/2 teaspoon (2 ml) baking powder
       1/2 teaspoon (2 ml) salt
       1/3 cup (75 ml) unsweetened cocoa
           1 teaspoon (5 ml) ground cinnamon
       1/2 teaspoon (2 ml) ground cloves
       1/3 cup (75 ml) semisweet chocolate
                pieces
           Confectioners sugar

Preheat oven to 325°F (160°C). Assemble Salad Maker with Shredder Disc and large bowl. Process zucchini (you should have 2 cups or 500 ml); set aside. Assemble Mixer. In large mixer bowl, cream butter, oil, and sugar at MEDIUM-LOW. Add eggs, vanilla extract, and sour cream; beat well at MEDIUM-LOW. Add flour, baking soda, baking powder, salt, cocoa, cinnamon, and cloves; mix at LOW until flour is moistened then at MEDIUM-LOW until well mixed, adding zucchini near the end. Pour batter into a greased 13×9×2-inch (33×23×5 cm) baking pan. Sprinkle chocolate pieces over top. Bake in preheated oven 40 to 45 minutes, or until toothpick inserted near center comes out clean. Cool in pan on rack. Sift confectioners sugar over top.

12 servings

Date Cake

A deliciously moist cake that is a good choice for a picnic.

       1/2 cup (125 ml) pecans
       1/2 pound (227 g) pitted dates
   1 1/2 cups (375 ml) water
   1 1/2 teaspoons (7 ml) baking soda
   1 1/2 cups (375 ml) sugar
       1/2 cup (125 ml) solid shortening
       1/2 teaspoon (2 ml) vanilla extract
           2 eggs
   1 2/3 cups (400 ml) all-purpose flour
       1/2 teaspoon (2 ml) salt
           1 package (6 ounces or 170 g)
                semisweet chocolate pieces

Assemble Food Grinder with Fine Disc. Grind nuts into small bowl; set aside. Grind dates. Combine dates and water in saucepan. Bring to boil, reduce heat and simmer 2 minutes; cool. Preheat oven to 350°F (180°C). Add 1 teaspoon (5 ml) baking soda to date mixture; stir. Assemble Mixer. In large mixer bowl, cream 1 cup (250 ml) sugar, shortening, and vanilla extract at MEDIUM-LOW. Add eggs, one at a time, beating well after each addition. Blend flour, remaining baking soda, and salt. Add dry ingredients alternately with date mixture, mixing at MEDIUM-LOW until mixed. Pour into a greased 8×8×2-inch (20×20×5 cm) baking pan. Mix chocolate pieces, remaining sugar, and chopped nuts; sprinkle over batter in pan. Bake in preheated oven for 40 to 50 minutes. Cool before serving.

16 servings

Pumpkin Cake

Butter Cream Cheese Frosting is the suggested frosting for this moist, spicy cake.

> 1 can (16 ounces or 454 g) pumpkin
> 2 cups (500 ml) all-purpose flour
> 2 teaspoons (10 ml) baking powder
> 1 teaspoon (5 ml) baking soda
> 1/2 teaspoon (2 ml) salt
> 1 teaspoon (5 ml) ground cinnamon
> 1/2 teaspoon (2 ml) ground nutmeg
> 1 cup (250 ml) sugar
> 1 cup (250 ml) firmly packed
>   brown sugar
> 4 eggs
> 1 cup (250 ml) vegetable oil

Assemble Mixer. In large mixer bowl, add all ingredients in order listed and mix at LOW until flour is moistened then at MEDIUM until smooth. Pour into a greased 13×9×2-inch (33×23×5 cm) baking pan. Bake at 350°F (180°C) for 45 minutes, or until toothpick inserted near center comes out clean. Cool thoroughly and frost with Butter Cream Cheese Frosting below.

12 servings

Butter Cream Cheese Frosting

This frosting is especially good on spice cakes and cakes with fruit.

> 1 package (8 ounces or 227 g)
>   cream cheese, at room
>   temperature
> 1/4 cup (50 ml) butter or margarine,
>   at room temperature
> 3 cups (750 ml) confectioners sugar
> 1 teaspoon (5 ml) vanilla extract

Assemble Mixer. In small mixer bowl, cream cream cheese and butter at MEDIUM-LOW. Add sugar and vanilla extract. Mix at LOW until sugar is moistened then at MEDIUM until smooth. Use to frost Hawaiian Fruit Cake (page 137) and Pumpkin Cake (opposite).

Enough frosting for a 13×9-inch (33×23 cm) cake

Heavenly Angel Food Cake

The mixer makes short work of preparing this tender and light angel food cake.

> 1 cup (250 ml) sifted cake flour
> 1 3/4 cups (450 ml) sugar
> 1 1/2 cups (375 ml) egg whites (1 dozen eggs),
>   at room temperature
> 1/2 teaspoon (2 ml) salt
> 1 1/2 teaspoons (7 ml) cream of tartar
> 1 teaspoon (5 ml) vanilla extract
> 1/2 teaspoon (2 ml) almond extract

Preheat oven to 375°F (190°C). Sift flour and 3/4 cup (200 ml) sugar together twice; set aside. Assemble Mixer. In large mixer bowl, beat egg whites and salt at MEDIUM-LOW then at HIGH for about 1 minute, or until whites barely hold peaks and are still very moist and slightly foamy. Sprinkle cream of tartar and extracts over egg whites. Beating at HIGH, add 1 cup (250 ml) sugar in 2-tablespoon (30 ml) portions. Beat until mixture holds a peak but tip of peak folds over. With rubber spatula, scrape sides of bowl. Sift all of flour-sugar mixture over top of batter. Fold mixture at LOW. Pour batter into ungreased 10-inch (25 cm) tube pan. Cut through batter with rubber spatula. Bake in preheated oven for 40 minutes. Invert cake and let cake cool completely before removing from pan.

One 10-inch (25 cm) tube cake

Holiday Orange Cake

This special dessert is filled with candied fruit and citrus zest.

    1 orange
    1 lemon
    2 cups (500 ml) sugar
  3/4 cup (200 ml) solid shortening
    2 eggs
2 1/2 cups (625 ml) all-purpose flour
    2 teaspoons (10 ml) baking soda
    1 cup (250 ml) buttermilk
    1 package (6 ounces or 170 g) mixed
       candied fruit

Preheat oven to 325°F (160°C). Assemble Citrus Juicer. Juice orange and measure 1/4 cup (50 ml). Juice lemon and measure 1/4 cup (50 ml). Set aside. Remove outer peel from orange and lemon. Assemble Blender. Put 1/2 cup (125 ml) sugar and the peel into blender container. Cover and process at CHOP until peel is minced; set aside. Assemble Mixer. In large mixer bowl, cream 1/2 cup (125 ml) sugar, shortening, and eggs at MEDIUM-LOW; add sugar-peel mixture and mix in well at MEDIUM-LOW. Combine flour and baking soda. Alternately add flour mixture and buttermilk to the creamed mixture mixing at MEDIUM-LOW until blended. Fold in candied fruit at LOW. Pour into greased 9×2-inch (23×5 cm) springform pan with tube insert. Bake in preheated oven for 1 hour or until toothpick inserted near center comes out clean. Pour reserved juice into small saucepan, add remaining 1 cup (25 ml) sugar, and boil over low heat. Cool cake for 10 minutes and remove from pan onto serving plate. Pour syrup over cake.

16 servings

Angel Cake Torte

Here is a party dessert to have ready in the refrigerator.

    1 cup (250 ml) whole blanched
       almonds
    1 envelope (1/4 ounce or 7 g)
       unflavored gelatin
    2 tablespoons (30 ml) boiling water
    4 eggs, separated
  1/8 teaspoon (0.5 ml) salt
  1/2 cup (125 ml) butter, at room
       temperature
    1 cup (250 ml) confectioners sugar
  1/4 cup (50 ml) rum or brandy
    1 10-inch (25 cm) angel food cake
       (see Heavenly Angel Food
       Cake, page 143)
    2 cups (500 ml) whipping cream

Assemble Blender. Put almonds into blender container. Cover and process 2 cycles at GRIND to chop nuts; set aside. Dissolve gelatin in boiling water. Assemble Mixer. In small mixer bowl, beat egg whites and salt at HIGH until stiff but not dry. Set aside. In large mixer bowl, cream butter, sugar, and egg yolks at MEDIUM-LOW until blended. Add dissolved gelatin, rum, and chopped almonds; mix at LOW just until mixed. Fold in beaten egg whites at LOW; chill until thickened. Slice cake into 3 crosswise sections. Spread filling between layers. Chill several hours before serving. In small mixer bowl, whip cream at LOW then at HIGH until stiff. Frost cake with whipped cream.

12 to 16 servings

Date Sauce

Spoon over cake squares or wedges.

- 1 **cup (250 ml) hot water**
- 1 **cup (250 ml) dates, pitted**
- 1/2 **cup (125 ml) sugar**
- 2 **tablespoons (30 ml) all-purpose flour**

Assemble Blender. Put all ingredients into blender container. Cover and process at GRIND 3 or 4 cycles until dates are chopped. Pour into small saucepan and slowly bring to a boil and stir over medium heat for 1 minute. Pour over hot Graham Cracker Cake (below).

About 2 cups (500 ml)

Graham Cracker Cake

An unusual cake that contains graham crackers instead of flour and is topped with Date Sauce.

- 45 **square graham crackers (about 2/3 pound or 303 g)**
- 1 1/2 **cups (375 ml) sugar**
- 2 **eggs**
- 1 **teaspoon (5 ml) vinegar**
- 1 **teaspoon (5 ml) baking soda**
- 1/2 **teaspoon (2 ml) salt**
- 2 **tablespoons (30 ml) vegetable oil**
- 1 1/2 **cups (375 ml) buttermilk**

Preheat oven to 350°F (180°C). Assemble Salad Maker with Shredder Disc and large mixer bowl. Process graham crackers. Assemble Mixer. Add remaining ingredients to bowl. Mix at LOW increasing to MEDIUM-HIGH until blended. Pour into greased 13×9×2-inch (33×23×5 cm) baking pan. Bake in preheated oven for 40 minutes, or until toothpick inserted near center comes out clean. While cake is

baking, prepare Date Sauce (opposite). Pour sauce over hot cake. Cool before serving.

12 to 16 servings

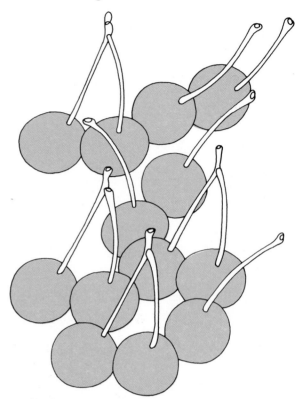

Spiced Maraschino Frosting

Use to frost spice as well as plain cake.

- 15 **large maraschino cherries**
- 1/3 **cup (75 ml) butter or margarine, at room temperature**
- 2 **cups (500 ml) confectioners sugar**
- 1/2 **teaspoon (2 ml) ground cinnamon**
- 1/8 **teaspoon (0.5 ml) ground nutmeg**
- 1/8 **teaspoon (0.5 ml) ground cloves**
- 3 **tablespoons (45 ml) light cream or half-and-half**

Assemble Mixer. In small mixer bowl, mix all ingredients except cherries at LOW. Add cherries and mix at MEDIUM-LOW until blended.

Enough frosting for a 9-inch (23 cm) square cake

Peanut Butter Frosting

Use as a frosting for yellow or chocolate cake.

- 3/4 cup (200 ml) confectioners sugar
- 1/4 cup (50 ml) butter, at room temperature
- 1/4 cup (50 ml) peanut butter, at room temperature
- 1 tablespoon (15 ml) milk

Assemble Mixer. In small mixer bowl, beat all ingredients at LOW then at MEDIUM-HIGH until sugar is dissolved.

Enough frosting for an 8-inch (20 cm) square cake

Cheesecake Cupcakes

Individual cheesecakes are fun to serve for dessert or a late evening snack.

- 24 vanilla wafers
- 2 packages (8 ounces or 227 g each) cream cheese, at room temperature
- 1 cup (250 ml) sugar
- 3 eggs
- 2 tablespoons (30 ml) lemon juice
- 1 teaspoon (5 ml) vanilla extract
- 1 can (21 ounces or 595 g) blueberry pie filling

Preheat oven to 375°F (190°C). Line two 12-cup muffin pans with foil baking cups. Put one cookie into each cup. Assemble Mixer. In large mixer bowl, cream cheese and sugar at MEDIUM-LOW. Add remaining ingredients, except pie filling and mix at LOW then at HIGH until smooth. Fill baking cups one-half full. Bake in preheated oven for 15 to 20 minutes. Cool and top each with a spoonful of pie filling.

24 cupcakes

Velvety Lemon Sauce

Pour over servings of cake.

- 2 strips lemon peel (about 2×1/4-inch or 5×0.6 cm)
- 1/2 cup (125 ml) sugar
- 1/4 cup (50 ml) cornstarch
- 1 1/3 cups (325 ml) water
- 3 tablespoons (45 ml) butter
- 1/4 cup (50 ml) lemon juice

Put lemon peel, sugar, and cornstarch into "Mini-Blend" container and process 2 or 3 cycles at MIX, or until lemon peel is finely chopped. Pour into a 1-quart (1 liter) saucepan and add remaining ingredients. Bring to a boil over medium heat, stirring constantly. Remove from heat. Serve while warm over Buttery Loaf Cake on page 140.

2 cups (500 ml)

Cherry Dessert Sauce

Serve over pudding as well as cake.

- 1/2 cup (125 ml) sugar
- 1 tablespoon (15 ml) all-purpose flour
- 1/4 teaspoon (1 ml) salt
- 3/4 cup (200 ml) water
- 1/8 teaspoon (0.5 ml) vanilla or almond extract
- 2 tablespoons (30 ml) butter or margarine, at room temperature
- 1 can (16 ounces or 454 g) red tart pitted cherries, drained

Assemble Blender. Put all ingredients except cherries into blender container. Cover and process at MIX until blended. Pour into a saucepan and heat slowly to boiling. Stir in cherries. Serve warm over Lemon-Lime Soda Cake on page 140.

About 2 cups (500 ml)

Cream Cheese Glaze

Use when a confectioners sugar glaze is needed.

    1 package (8 ounces or 227 g)
        cream cheese, at room
        temperature
1 1/3 cups (325 ml) confectioners sugar
    1 tablespoon (15 ml) light cream
        or half-and-half

Assemble Mixer. In small mixer bowl, put all ingredients and beat at LOW until blended then at HIGH until smooth and spreading consistency. Use to frost Apple Carrot Cake on page 138.

Enough frosting for 13 × 9-inch (33 × 23 cm) cake.

Butterscotch Brownies

These cookie squares have double butterscotch flavor.

    1/3 cup (75 ml) butter or margarine
      1 cup (250 ml) firmly packed brown sugar
    1/2 cup (125 ml) pecans
      2 eggs
1 1/2 teaspoons (7 ml) vanilla extract
      1 cup (250 ml) all-purpose flour
      1 teaspoon (5 ml) baking powder
    1/2 teaspoon (2 ml) salt
      1 package (6 ounces or 170 g)
          butterscotch-flavored pieces
          Confectioners sugar

Melt butter in medium saucepan and stir in brown sugar. Pour into small mixer bowl; cool to room temperature. Preheat oven to 350°F (180°C). Put pecans into "Mini-Blend" container and process 2 cycles at WHIP to chop nuts; set aside.

Assemble Mixer. Add eggs, vanilla extract, and dry ingredients to cooled mixture and mix at LOW then at MEDIUM-HIGH until well mixed. Stir in butterscotch pieces and nuts. Spread in a greased 8×8×2-inch (20×20×5 cm) baking pan. Bake in preheated oven for 30 to 35 minutes. Sprinkle with confectioners sugar. Cut into squares.

16 cookies

Banana Brownies

A new and delicious version of brownies for dessert as well as a snack.

    1/4 cup (50 ml) butter or margarine,
          at room temperature
      2 ripe bananas, sliced
      1 egg
1 1/2 cups (375 ml) all-purpose flour
    3/4 cup (200 ml) sugar
      1 teaspoon (5 ml) ground cinnamon
    1/2 teaspoon (2 ml) baking powder
    1/4 teaspoon (1 ml) baking soda
    1/4 teaspoon (1 ml) salt
    1/2 cup (125 ml) buttermilk
      1 cup (250 ml) semisweet chocolate
          pieces

Preheat oven to 350°F (180°C). Assemble Mixer. In large mixer bowl, mix all ingredients except chocolate pieces at LOW until dry ingredients are moistened then at MEDIUM until thoroughly combined. Stir in chocolate pieces. Pour into a greased 8×8×2-inch (20×20×5 cm) baking pan. Bake in preheated oven for 40 minutes. Cool before cutting into squares.

25 cookies

Date Bars

These moist and nutty bars keep well refrigerated or frozen.

    3 eggs
    1 cup (250 ml) dates, pitted
    1 cup (250 ml) walnuts
    1 cup (250 ml) sugar
  1/2 cup (125 ml) all-purpose flour
    1 teaspoon (5 ml) baking powder
  1/2 teaspoon (2 ml) salt
    1 teaspoon (5 ml) vanilla extract
       Confectioners sugar for coating

Assemble Blender. Put eggs, dates, and nuts into blender container. Cover and process 3 or 4 cycles at GRIND, or until dates and nuts are chopped. Assemble Mixer. In small mixer bowl, mix date mixture and remaining ingredients at LOW until dry ingredients are moistened, then at MEDIUM until mixed. Spread in a greased 9-inch (23 cm) square baking pan. Bake at 350°F (180°C) for 35 to 45 minutes. Cool thoroughly and cut into bars. Roll bars in confectioners sugar.

40 cookies

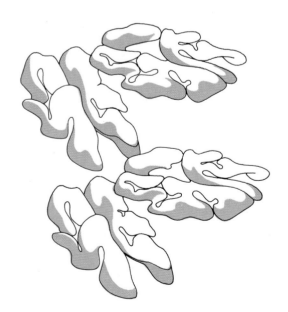

Frosted Chocolate Cake Bars

Decorate the top with chopped nuts as desired.

    1 cup (250 ml) butter or margarine
  1/3 cup (75 ml) unsweetened cocoa
    1 cup (250 ml) water
    2 cups (500 ml) all-purpose flour
    2 cups (500 ml) sugar
    2 eggs, slightly beaten
  1/2 cup (125 ml) buttermilk
    1 teaspoon (5 ml) baking soda
    1 teaspoon (5 ml) vanilla extract

Frosting:

  1/2 cup (125 ml) butter or margarine,
         melted
    3 tablespoons (45 ml) unsweetened cocoa
    6 tablespoons (90 ml) buttermilk
    1 teaspoon (5 ml) vanilla extract
    4 cups (1 liter) confectioners sugar

Preheat oven to 350°F (180°C). Grease and flour a 15 1/2 × 10 1/2 × 1-inch (39 × 27 × 3 cm) jelly roll pan; set aside. Heat butter, cocoa, and water to a boil in 1-quart (1 liter) saucepan. Assemble Mixer. In large mixer bowl, put flour and sugar; add hot cocoa mixture. Mix at LOW until dry ingredients are moistened; then mix at MEDIUM-LOW; add eggs, buttermilk, baking soda, and vanilla. Mix well at LOW. Pour into prepared pan. Bake in preheated oven for 30 minutes, or until toothpick inserted near center comes out clean. Let stand for 10 minutes. In small mixer bowl, put ingredients for frosting and mix at LOW until sugar is moistened then at MEDIUM-LOW until smooth and spreadable. Spread frosting over warm cake. Cool and cut into bars.

48 bars

Brown Sugar Crisps

This easy-to-mix dough does not need chilling before rolling and cutting into shapes.

   2 cups (500 ml) firmly packed
        brown sugar
   1 cup (250 ml) solid shortening
   2 eggs
   1 tablespoon (15 ml) water
   4 cups (1 liter) all-purpose flour
   1 teaspoon (5 ml) baking soda
   3/4 teaspoon (3 ml) salt

Preheat oven to 375°F (190°C). Assemble Mixer. In large mixer bowl, cream sugar, shortening, eggs, and water at MEDIUM-LOW until fluffy. Add 2 cups (500 ml) flour, baking soda, and salt to mixture and mix at LOW until flour is moistened then at MEDIUM until smooth. Add remaining flour and mix at LOW then at MEDIUM. The dough should be smooth and pliable. Do not chill dough. Roll out dough 1/8-inch (0.3 cm) thick on lightly floured surface. Cut into circles or other shapes. Put onto ungreased cookie sheets. Bake in preheated oven for 8 to 10 minutes, or until lightly browned. Remove from cookie sheets while hot. Cool on racks.

6 dozen cookies

Variation: Add 1 cup (250 ml) chopped coconut along with first half of flour.

Peanut Butter Oatmeal Cookies

Chewy oatmeal and creamy peanut butter make these cookies a delicious lunchbox treat.

   1/2 cup (125 ml) butter or margarine,
          at room temperature
   1/2 cup (125 ml) peanut butter, at room
          temperature
   1/2 cup (125 ml) sugar
   1/2 cup (125 ml) firmly packed
          brown sugar
     1 egg
     1 teaspoon (5 ml) vanilla extract
     1 cup (250 ml) quick-cooking
          rolled oats
     1 cup (250 ml) all-purpose flour
   3/4 teaspoon (3 ml) baking soda
   1/4 teaspoon (1 ml) salt

Preheat oven to 375°F (190°C). Assemble Mixer. In large mixer bowl, cream butter, peanut butter, and sugars at MEDIUM-LOW. Add remaining ingredients. Mix on LOW until dry ingredients are moistened then at MEDIUM-LOW until smooth. Drop by teaspoonfuls onto greased cookie sheets. Flatten in crisscross fashion with a floured fork. Bake in preheated oven for 8 to 10 minutes. Cool on racks.

4 dozen cookies

Peanut Butter Cookies, Mom's Molasses Cookies (page 152), Brown Sugar Cookies

Texas Cookies

This crunchy cookie hits the spot as a breakfast treat or mid-afternoon pick-me-up.

  1 cup (250 ml) solid shortening
1/2 cup (125 ml) sugar
  1 cup (250 ml) firmly packed
      brown sugar
  2 eggs
  1 teaspoon (5 ml) vanilla extract
  2 cups (500 ml) all-purpose flour
  1 teaspoon (5 ml) baking soda
  1 teaspoon (5 ml) baking powder
1/2 teaspoon (2 ml) salt
  1 cup (250 ml) seedless raisins
  2 cups (500 ml) corn flakes

Preheat oven to 350°F (180°C). Assemble Mixer. In large mixer bowl, cream shortening, sugars, eggs, and vanilla extract at MEDIUM-LOW. Add remaining ingredients except raisins and corn flakes and mix at LOW until flour is moistened then at MEDIUM until well mixed. Stir in raisins and cornflakes on LOW. Drop by teaspoonfuls onto greased cookie sheets. Bake in preheated oven for 12 to 15 minutes. Cool on racks.

4 dozen cookies

Mom's Molasses Cookies

These spicy molasses cookies may well become a family favorite.

    1 cup (250 ml) molasses
    1 cup (250 ml) sugar
    1 cup (250 ml) solid shortening
    1 egg
4 1/2 cups (1125 ml) all-purpose flour
    1 teaspoon (5 ml) baking soda
    1 teaspoon (5 ml) ground cinnamon
    1 teaspoon (5 ml) ground cloves
    1 teaspoon (5 ml) ground ginger
  1/4 cup (50 ml) cold coffee

Assemble Mixer. In large mixer bowl, beat molasses, sugar, shortening, and egg at MEDIUM-LOW until blended. Add remaining ingredients and mix at LOW then at MEDIUM until well mixed. Cover bowl and refrigerate overnight. Preheat oven to 400°F (200°C). Roll out dough, a portion at a time, on floured board; add only enough flour to make dough easy to handle. Roll to 1/4-inch (0.6 cm) thickness. Cut out rounds and put on greased cookie sheets. Bake in preheated oven for 7 minutes, or until light browned and set. Remove cookies while hot and cool on racks. Store in airtight container. If soft cookies are preferred, add a slice of bread to container of cookies.

6 1/2 dozen 3-inch (8 cm) cookies

Granola Cookies

These soft, chewy raisin cookies have a touch of cinnamon.

  1/2 cup (125 ml) butter or margarine,
        at room temperature
  1/4 cup (50 ml) honey
    1 egg
    1 teaspoon (5 ml) vanilla extract
  3/4 cup (200 ml) whole wheat flour
  1/2 teaspoon (2 ml) baking soda
  1/2 teaspoon (2 ml) salt
  1/2 teaspoon (2 ml) ground cinnamon
1 1/2 cups (375 ml) granola
    1 cup (250 ml) seedless raisins

Preheat oven to 350°F (180°C). Assemble Mixer. In large mixer bowl, mix all ingredients at LOW then at MEDIUM until well mixed. Drop by teaspoonfuls onto ungreased cookie sheets. Bake in preheated oven for 8 to 10 minutes. Cool thoroughly on rack before storing.

About 30 cookies

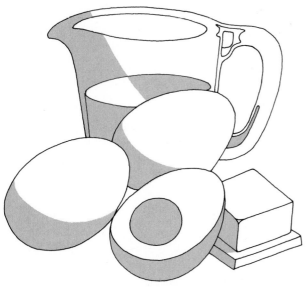

Sesame Oatmeal Cookies

These wholesome cookies make a fine after-school snack.

1	egg
1/4	cup (50 ml) milk
1/3	cup (75 ml) vegetable oil
1/3	cup (75 ml) honey
3/4	cup (200 ml) pitted dates
1	cup (250 ml) whole wheat flour
1 1/2	cups (375 ml) quick-cooking rolled oats
1/3	cup (75 ml) soy flour
1/2	teaspoon (2 ml) salt
1	teaspoon (5 ml) ground cinnamon
3/4	cup (200 ml) sesame seed

Preheat oven to 375°F (190°C). Assemble Blender. Put egg, milk, oil, honey, and dates into blender container. Cover and process 4 cycles at GRIND or until dates are chopped. Assemble Mixer. In large mixer bowl, put date mixture and remaining ingredients. Mix at MEDIUM-LOW until mixed. Drop by teaspoonfuls onto well-greased cookie sheets. Bake in preheated oven for 8 to 10 minutes or until edges are golden brown. Cool thoroughly on racks before storing.

3 to 3 1/2 dozen cookies

Choco-Chip Oatmeal Cookies

These soft, chewy cookies are ideal for the lunch bag.

1	cup (250 ml) walnuts
1	cup (250 ml) solid shortening
3/4	cup (200 ml) firmly packed brown sugar
3/4	cup (200 ml) honey
2	eggs
1	teaspoon (5 ml) vanilla extract
3/4	cup (200 ml) milk
2	cups (500 ml) all-purpose flour
1	teaspoon (5 ml) baking soda
1/4	teaspoon (1 ml) salt
4	cups (1 liter) quick-cooking rolled oats
1	package (6 ounces or 170 g) semisweet chocolate pieces

Assemble Blender. Put walnuts into blender container. Cover and process 2 cycles at WHIP to chop nuts; set aside. Assemble Mixer. In large mixer bowl, cream shortening, sugar, and honey at MEDIUM-LOW until fluffy. Add eggs and mix at MEDIUM-LOW until blended. Add vanilla extract and milk and mix at MEDIUM-LOW until blended. Add flour, baking soda, and salt; mix at LOW until flour is moistened then at MEDIUM. Mix in oats, chocolate pieces, and nuts at MEDIUM-LOW until mixed. Cover bowl and chill overnight. Preheat oven to 350°F (180°C). Drop batter by tablespoonfuls onto greased cookie sheet. Bake for 12 to 14 minutes, or until lightly browned. Remove cookies while hot from cookie sheets; cool on wire racks. Store in airtight container.

9 dozen cookies

Standard Pastry

Prepare pastry baked or unbaked as directed in recipes.

>   1   cup (250 ml) all-purpose flour
> 1/3   cup (75 ml) solid shortening
> 1/2   teaspoon (2 ml) salt
>   2   to 3 tablespoons (30 to 45 ml)
>   cold water

Assemble Mixer. In large mixer bowl, mix all ingredients except water at LOW until mixture resembles coarse meal. Add water, 1 tablespoon (15 ml) at a time, mixing as little as possible and only until dough holds together. Shape into a ball. Roll out on floured pastry cloth. Fit pastry into an 8- or 9-inch (20 to 23 cm) pie pan and flute edges. (If pie shell is to be baked, prick pastry thoroughly with a fork and bake in preheated 475°F (250°C) oven for 8 to 10 minutes. Cool on rack.)

One 8- to 9-inch (20 to 23 cm) shell

Variations: Pastry for 2-Crust Pie: Follow recipe for Standard Pastry, doubling ingredients. Divide pastry in two portions and shape into balls. Roll out one pastry ball 1-inch (2.5 cm) larger than overall size of pie pan. Gently fold pastry in half and set aside. Roll out second pastry ball and gently fit pastry into pie pan. Add filling, moisten edge, and cover with top crust; seal and flute edge. Make steam holes in top. Bake as directed.

Pastry for Lattice-Top Pie: Follow recipe for Pastry for 2-Crust Pie. Roll one pastry ball for bottom crust; fit into pie pan. Roll second pastry ball into a rectangle. Cut pastry into strips with sharp knife or pastry wheel. Add filling to pie shell. Form a lattice pattern on top with pastry strips. Bake as directed.

Graham Cracker Crumb Crust

The ingredients for crumb crusts can be mixed in the pie pan or in a bowl.

>   Graham crackers (10 to 12 squares)
> 1/3   cup (75 ml) melted butter
>   2   tablespoons (30 ml) sugar
> 1/2   teaspoon (2 ml) ground cinnamon

Assemble Salad Maker with Shredder Disc and large bowl. Process enough graham crackers to measure 1 cup (250 ml) crumbs. Put crumbs and remaining ingredients into a 9-inch (23 cm) pie pan. Mix thoroughly. Pat onto bottom and sides of pan. Chill before filling or bake in preheated 350°F (180°C) oven for 10 minutes and let cool before filling.

One 9-inch (23 cm) crust

Variations: Chocolate Cookie Crust: Follow recipe for Graham Cracker Crumb Crust; substitute 1 package (8 1/2 ounces or 227 g) chocolate cookies for graham crackers and process cookies. Omit sugar.

Gingersnap Crumb Crust: Follow recipe for Graham Cracker Crumb Crust; substitute 1 cup (250 ml) gingersnap crumbs for graham cracker crumbs, reduce sugar to 2 teaspoons (10 ml), and omit cinnamon.

Pretzel Crumb Crust: Follow recipe for Graham Cracker Crumb Crust; substitute 1 cup (250 ml) pretzel crumbs for graham cracker crumbs. Reduce sugar to 1 teaspoon (5 ml) and omit cinnamon. Fill with ice cream, if desired.

Vanilla Wafer Crumb Crust: Follow recipe for Graham Cracker Crumb Crust; substitute 1 cup (250 ml) vanilla wafer crumbs for graham cracker crumbs and reduce sugar to 2 teaspoons (10 ml).

Fresh Peach Pie

The custard layer forms a pretty topping for the peaches in this pie.

> 6 large ripe peaches
> 1 unbaked 9-inch (23cm) pie shell (see Standard Pastry, page 154)
> 1 tablespoon (15 ml) quick-cooking tapicoa
> 1 cup (250 ml) sugar
> 1 teaspoon (5 ml) ground cinnamon
> 4 egg yolks
> 1/4 cup (50 ml) light cream or half-and-half

Peel, halve, and pit peaches. Assemble Salad Maker with Thick Slicer Disc and large bowl. Process peaches; set aside. Sprinkle one half of tapioca on bottom of pie shell. Mix remaining tapioca, 3/4 cup (200 ml) sugar, and cinnamon; sprinkle over peaches as they are put into pie shell. Assemble Mixer. In small mixer bowl, mix remaining sugar, egg yolks, and cream at MEDIUM until sugar is dissolved. Pour over peaches. Bake in preheated 425°F (220°C) oven for 15 minutes, then at 350°F (180°C) for 15 minutes.

One 9-inch (23 cm) pie

Frozen Apples in Syrup

A convenient short cut for pie filling or top with a dollop of whipped cream for a quick dessert.

> 4 3/4 cups (1.2 liters) sugar
> 4 cups (1 liter) water
> 12 pounds (5.5 kg) apples, cored and pared

Measure sugar and water into saucepan; cook until sugar dissolves. Cool. Prepare canning jars and lids for freezing. Select full-flavored apples that are crisp and firm, not mealy in texture. Assemble Salad Maker with Thick Slicer Disc. Process apples. To prevent darkening, place sliced apples in a solution of 8 cups water and 4 teaspoons (20 ml) commercial ascorbic acid mixture. Drain apples. Pour 1/2 cup (125 ml) cold syrup into jars. Press apple slices down in jars and add enough syrup to cover, leaving 1/4-inch (.6 cm) head space. Remove air bubbles with non-metallic kitchen utensil. Adjust caps, label and freeze.

9 pints (4.5 liters)

Sweet Potato Pie

Serve this colorful fresh sweet potato pie with whipped cream, if desired.

> 2 pounds (907 g) sweet potatoes
> 3 eggs
> 3/4 cup (200 ml) light corn syrup
> 1/4 cup (50 ml) firmly packed brown sugar
> 1/4 cup (50 ml) butter or margarine, at room temperature
> 1 teaspoon (5 ml) vanilla extract
> 1/8 teaspoon (0.5 ml) salt
> 1 cup (250 ml) pecan halves
> 1 unbaked 9-inch (23 cm) pie shell (see Standard Pastry, page 154)

Cook sweet potatoes covered in saucepan with water until tender. Drain. Assemble Puréer. Process sweet potatoes at HIGH (about 1 1/2 cups or 375 ml). Preheat oven to 350°F (180°C). Assemble Blender. Put all ingredients except 1/2 cup (125 ml) pecans and pie shell into blender container. Cover and process at GRIND until well mixed. Pour into pie shell and decorate with remaining pecans. Bake in preheated oven for 1 hour, or until knife inserted in center comes out clean.

6 to 8 servings

Strawberry Bavarian Pie

Europeans are noted for their rich desserts and this pie is no exception. With beautiful fluffy texture and the sweet taste of strawberries, this dessert is sure to be a universal favorite.

Crust:

- 1/2 cup (125 ml) walnuts
- 1/2 cup (125 ml) butter, at room temperature
- 2 tablespoons (30 ml) sugar
- 1 egg yolk
- 1 cup (250 ml) all-purpose flour

Filling:

- 1 package (10 ounces or 284 g) frozen strawberries, thawed and drained
- 2 egg whites
- 1 cup (250 ml) sugar
- 1/2 teaspoon (2 ml) almond extract
- 1/4 teaspoon (1 ml) salt
- 1 cup (250 ml) whipping cream

For crust, preheat oven to 400°F (200°C). Put walnuts into "Mini-Blend" container and process 2 or 3 cycles at GRIND, or until nuts are finely chopped. Assemble Mixer. In small mixer bowl, mix nuts, butter, sugar, egg yolk, and flour at LOW then at MEDIUM-LOW until thoroughly mixed. Using spatula, spread mixture on bottom and sides of a 10×1 1/2-inch (25×4 cm) pie pan. Bake in preheated oven for 12 minutes. Cool thoroughly. For filling, in large mixer bowl, beat all ingredients except whipping cream at MEDIUM-HIGH until very thick and double in volume (10 to 15 minutes). Set aside. In clean small mixer bowl with clean beaters, whip cream at LOW then at HIGH until stiff. Fold cream into strawberry mixture with rubber spatula until blended. Pour into pie shell and swirl top with spoon. Put uncovered into freezer and freeze until firm. (If necessary to store, wrap securely with foil.) About 1 hour before serving, put pie into refrigerator to soften.

8 servings

Two-Crust Apple Pie

Choose apples for baking such as Rome Beauty, Jonathan, or Golden Delicious.

- 4 or 5 baking apples, quartered, pared, and cored
- 1 tablespoon (15 ml) lemon juice
- 3/4 cup (200 ml) sugar
- 1 1/2 tablespoons (23 ml) all-purpose flour
- 1/4 teaspoon (1 ml) salt
- 1/4 teaspoon (1 ml) ground cinnamon
  Pastry for 2-crust 9-inch (23 cm) pie (page 154); use lattice top, if desired
- 1 tablespoon (15 ml) butter or margarine

Assemble Salad Maker with Thick Slicer Disc and large bowl. Process apples and sprinkle with lemon juice. Mix sugar, flour, salt, and cinnamon. Add to apple slices and toss. Prepare pastry and line a 9-inch (23 cm) pie plate. Fill pie shell with sugared apple slices. Dot with butter. Cover with top crust; seal and flute edge. Make steam holes in top. Bake in preheated 400°F (200°C) oven for 40 minutes, or until apples are tender.

One 9-inch (23 cm) pie

Mocha Crunch Dessert

This can be prepared and served in minutes with your blender.

- **2 cups (500 ml) cold milk**
- **1 package (3 3/4 ounces or 106 g) instant vanilla pudding**
- **2 tablespoons (30 ml) instant coffee granules**
- **2 bars (1 1/8 ounces or 31.8 g each) chocolate covered toffee bars, broken in 1-inch (2.5 cm) pieces**
- **Whipped topping**

Assemble Blender. Put milk, pudding mix, and coffee in blender container. Cover and process at MIX until pudding begins to thicken. Add candy bars. Cover and process 2 to 3 cycles or until coarsely crushed. Pour into dessert or parfait glasses. Garnish with whipped topping.

4 servings

Fresh Applesauce

Serve the applesauce freshly made or chill before serving.

- **1/4 cup (50 ml) liquid (fruit juice or water)**
- **4 apples, cut in eighths (remove peel, if desired)**
- **1/4 cup (50 ml) sugar**
- **Dash ground cinnamon**

Assemble Blender. Put liquid and 4 or 5 pieces of apple into blender container. Cover and process at BLEND until smooth. Increase speed to LIQUEFY, with motor running, remove feeder cap and add remaining apples, a few at a time. Add sugar and cinnamon.

2 cups (500 ml)

Note: *If desired, add 2 teaspoons (10 ml) ascorbic acid powder to keep fruit from darkening.*

Frozen Applesauce: *Follow recipe for Fresh Applesauce, substituting 1/2 cup (125 ml) light corn syrup and 1/4 cup (50 ml) lemon juice for liquid and sugar. Pour into freezer container, allowing 1/2-inch (1.3 cm) headspace; cover. Freeze.*

Strawberry Ice Cream

This delicious ice cream is easily prepared and frozen in trays.

- **1 quart (1 liter) fresh strawberries**
- **1/2 cup (125 ml) sugar**
- **Dash salt**
- **4 eggs**
- **2 cups (500 ml) whipping cream**

Assemble Juice Extractor. Process strawberries at recommended speed. Measure 2 cups (500 ml) juice and 1/2 cup (125 ml) pulp. Set aside. Heat juice, sugar, and salt in 2-quart (2 liter) saucepan, stirring occasionally. Beat eggs in bowl, pour in 1/2 cup (125 ml) hot juice, and mix thoroughly. Stir slowly into juice in saucepan and continue heating over medium heat; stir constantly until thickened. Remove from heat. Chill thoroughly. Assemble Mixer. Beat whipping cream to soft peaks at HIGH. Fold cream and pulp into chilled custard mixture. Turn into ice cube trays without dividers or 13×9×2-inch (33×23×5 cm) pan. Freeze for 3 to 4 hours, or until firm.

1 quart (1 liter)

Frozen Ice Cream Dessert

A graham cracker crumb crust forms the base for this ice cream sundae dessert.

> **Graham Cracker Crumb Crust (page 154)**
> 1 **quart (1 liter) vanilla ice cream, softened**
> 3/4 **cup (200 ml) confectioners' sugar**
> 1/2 **cup (125 g) butter or margarine, at room temperature**
> 2 **eggs**
> 2 **squares (1 ounce or 28 g each) unsweetened chocolate, melted**
> 1 **teaspoon (5 ml) vanilla extract**

Put ingredients for crumb crust into an 8×8×2-inch (20×20×5 cm) pan, mix well, and press into a layer. Chill. Spoon softened ice cream into crust and spread evenly. Set in refrigerator. Assemble Mixer. In small mixer bowl, beat remaining ingredients at LOW then at HIGH until well mixed and fluffy. Spread over ice cream in pan. Freeze until firm.

8 to 12 servings

Caramel Cream Custard

Caramel syrup is the topping for these individual baked custards.

> 3/4 **cup (200 ml) sugar**
> 1 **tablespoon (15 ml) water**
> 3 **eggs**
> 1 **teaspoon (5 ml) vanilla extract**
> **Dash salt**
> 2 **cups (500 ml) hot milk**

Put 1/2 cup (125 ml) sugar and water into a heavy saucepan; cook over high heat until syrup becomes golden brown. Pour equal amounts of syrup into 6 individual custard cups. Assemble Blender. Put eggs, vanilla extract, salt, and remaining sugar into blender container. Cover and process at BEAT. While blender is running, remove feeder cap and slowly add hot milk. Process just until mixed. Pour mixture into prepared custard cups. Put cups into shallow pan containing 1-inch (2.5 cm) depth of water. (For the best results, put paper toweling in bottom of pan and set cups on paper; this prevents the custard from splitting or cracking.) Bake in preheated 350°F (180°C)) oven for 40 to 50 minutes, or until knife inserted in center comes out clean. Chill thoroughly; unmold and serve.

6 servings

Quick Gelatin Mold

Serve the gelatin plain, with fruit, or with whipped topping.

> 1 **package (3 ounces or 85 g) fruit-flavored gelatin**
> 1/2 **cup (125 ml) boiling water**
> 1 1/2 **cups (375 ml) crushed ice**

Assemble Blender. Put gelatin and boiling water into blender container. Cover and process at BEAT until gelatin is dissolved. Increase speed to LIQUEFY, remove feeder cap, and add crushed ice. Process until ice is liquefied and mixture begins to thicken. Pour into a 2-cup (500 ml) mold; chill for 5 minutes before unmolding. Or pour into serving dishes and chill for 5 minutes before serving.

4 to 6 servings

Sour Cream Apple Dessert

Serve this baked apple pudding warm, either plain or topped with ice cream.

    3 or 4 large baking apples
    3 tablespoons (45 ml) all-purpose flour
    3/4 cup (200 ml) sugar
    1/8 teaspoon (0.5 ml) salt
    1/2 teaspoon (2 ml) ground nutmeg
    1 egg
    1 teaspoon (5 ml) vanilla extract
    1 cup (250 ml) dairy sour cream

Topping:

    1/3 cup (75 ml) sugar
    1/3 cup (75 ml) all-purpose flour
    1 teaspoon (5 ml) ground cinnamon
    1/4 cup (50 ml) butter, at room temperature

Preheat oven to 350°F (180°C). Grease an 8×8×2-inch (20×20×5 cm) baking dish. Assemble Salad Maker with Thick Slicer Disc and large bowl. Quarter, pare, and core apples, then process apples; (about 4 cups or 1 liter); set aside. Assemble Mixer. In large mixer bowl, put all ingredients except apples and mix at LOW until smooth. Stir in apple slices. Pour into prepared dish. Bake in preheated oven for 20 minutes. Meanwhile, in small mixer bowl, mix ingredients for topping at LOW until blended. Spoon over apples. Bake for 20 minutes, or until apple slices are fork tender.

9 servings

Irish Coffee Dessert

A gourmet dessert in just minutes.

    2 envelopes (1/4-ounce or 7 g each) unflavored gelatin
    1 cup (250 ml) cold milk
    1 cup (250 ml) milk, heated to boiling
    2/3 cup (150 ml) sugar
    2 tablespoons (30 ml) instant coffee
    1 ounce (7 ml) Irish whisky
    1 ounce (7 ml) creme de cacao
    1 cup (250 ml) whipping cream
    6 to 8 ice cubes

Assemble Blender. Put cold milk in blender container and sprinkle gelatin over. Let stand 3 to 4 minutes. Add hot milk; cover and process at STIR until gelatin dissolves (about 2 minutes). Add sugar, coffee powder, whisky and liqueur. Cover and process at LIQUEFY until blended. With motor on, remove feeder cap, and add cream and ice cubes, one at a time. Replace cap and continue to process until ice is liquefied. Pour into mugs or dessert dishes and chill until set (about 30 minutes). Garnish with sweetened whipping cream and chocolate curls, if desired.

about 6 servings

The Good Old Days

When bushels of apples and ripe garden produce beckon you to preserve their goodness, turn to the Oster "Kitchen Center" unit for quick processing help. You'll be rewarded by jars of apple juice, pickles, and chutney in the pantry, a stock of fresh tomato sauce in the freezer and the delicious tastes of refrigerated Pear Honey and Raw Cranberry Relish.

Some tips for safe canning: Use only jars designed for canning; make sure they are free of knicks, cracks, and sharp edges that might interfere with the seal. Jars must be washed and warmed. Leave space for boiling water to circulate around jars in the water bath. Start counting processing time, according to the recipes, after the water has reached a steady, gentle boil. After jars have been removed and allowed to cool, check to be sure they are completely sealed; metal lids will be depressed in the centers and other types should not leak when inverted. If the seal is not complete, reheat the mixture to boiling and repack it, or store in refrigerator for immediate use.

Pear Honey

A special homemade treat to serve with bread or rolls.

- **4 ripe pears, pared, cored, and quartered**
- **1 lemon, seeded and quartered**
- **3 cups (750 ml) sugar**
- **1/4 teaspoon (1 ml) salt**
- **1/2 teaspoon (2 ml) ground nutmeg**

Assemble Blender. Put pears (about 2 cups or 500 ml) into blender container. Cover and process at GRIND until smooth. Add remaining ingredients and process at GRIND until lemon is finely chopped. Pour into 3-quart saucepan and bring to a boil over medium heat, stirring constantly. Reduce heat to medium and continue to cook for about 30 minutes, or until mixture is thick. Ladle into hot jelly jars and seal. Store in refrigerator.

3 cups (750 ml)

Cucumber Sandwich Pickles

Be sure to select firm, rather small cucumbers.

10 to 12 small to medium cucumbers

Mixture 1:
1/2 cup (125 ml) salt
2 quarts (2 liters) cold water

Mixture 2:
3 cups (750 ml) vinegar
3 cups (750 ml) water

Mixture 3:
2 cups (500 ml) vinegar
1 cup (250 ml) water
1 cup (250 ml) firmly packed
   brown sugar
1 cup (250 ml) sugar
1/2 teaspoon (2 ml) celery seed
1/2 teaspoon (2 ml) mustard seed
1/2 teaspoon (2 ml) ground turmeric

Wash cucumbers and remove blossom ends. Assemble Salad Maker with Thick Slicer Disc and large bowl. Process cucumbers. For Mixture 1, sprinkle cucumbers with salt, add cold water, and let stand for 2 to 3 hours. Drain thoroughly. Prepare jars and lids for canning. For Mixture 2, combine vinegar and water in large saucepan; bring to boiling. Add cucumbers; simmer about 8 minutes. (Cucumbers should not become soft.) Drain well, discarding liquid. For Mixture 3, combine vinegar and water with remaining ingredients; simmer for 10 minutes. add drained cucumbers. Bring to boiling. Carefully pack, boiling hot, into hot pint (500 ml) jars, leaving 1/4-inch (0.6 cm) head space. Remove air bubbles with non-metallic kitchen utensil. Adjust caps. Process in boiling water bath canner for 10 minutes. Remove jars and let cool on racks.

About 3 pints (1.5 liters)

Italian Cooking Sauce

Have this tasty homemade sauce ready to use for spaghetti, lasagna, manicotti, and other pasta dishes.

10 pounds (5 kg) ripe tomatoes,
   stems removed
2 tablespoons (30 ml) sugar
2 tablespoons (30 ml) dried
   Italian seasoning
1 tablespoon (15 ml) salt
1/4 teaspoon (1 ml) garlic powder
2 medium onions, quartered
1 green pepper, quartered
1 cup (250 ml) water
1/4 cup (50 ml) cornstarch
1/2 cup (125 ml) cold water

Assemble Puréer. Process tomatoes on HIGH into 5-quart (5 liter) saucepan. Add dry seasonings. Cook onion and green pepper covered in small saucepan with 1 cup (250 ml) water until tender. Purée. Add to saucepan with tomato purée; stir well. Simmer over medium heat until thickened (about 2 hours). Dissolve cornstarch in cold water. Add to sauce and bring to a boil, stirring constantly. Remove from heat. Allow to cool. Store in refrigerator or freeze up to 6 months in freezer containers.

2 quarts (2 liters)

Old-Fashioned Bread and Butter Pickles (page 164), Italian Cooking Sauce, Cucumber Sandwich Pickles

Apple Chutney

Serve as an accompaniment to main dishes especially curried ones.

 4   **pounds (1816 g) apples,
       quartered, pared, and cored**
 1   **cup (250 ml) pitted dates**
 1   **cup (250 ml) dried peaches**
 1   **cup (250 ml) dried pears**
 1 1/2   **cups (375 ml) raisins**
 1   **large onion, quartered**
 2   **cloves garlic**
 2   **cups (500 ml) cider vinegar**
 5 1/2   **cups (1275 ml) firmly packed
       brown sugar**
 3   **tablespoons (45 ml) salt**
 2   **teaspoons (10 ml) ground nutmeg**
 1   **teaspoon (5 ml) ground ginger**
 1/4   **teaspoon (1 ml) ground red pepper
       or cayenne pepper**
 4   **whole peppercorns**
 4   **whole cloves**

Assemble Food Grinder with Coarse Disc. Grind fruits, onion, and garlic into large kettle; add vinegar. Mix well. Cover and let stand 24 hours. Stir in sugar, 3 tablespoons (45 ml) salt, and spices. Simmer mixture until thick (about 1 hour), stirring occasionally. Ladle into sterilized jars and seal. Process for 10 minutes in boiling water bath canner. Remove jars and let cool on racks.

6 1/2 pints (3.3 liters)

Old-Fashioned Bread and Butter Pickles

These crisp, sweet-tart pickles are a welcome addition to a relish tray.

 50   **small to medium cucumbers**
 12   **to 15 onions (2 3/4 pounds
       or 1347 g)**
 1/2   **cup (125 ml) salt**
     Ice cubes
 1   **quart (1 liter) vinegar**
 4   **cups (1 liter) sugar**
 1   **tablespoon (15 ml) celery seed**
 2   **tablespoons (30 ml) mustard seed**
 1   **tablespoon (15 ml) ground ginger**

Assemble Salad Maker with Thick Slicer Disc and large bowl. Process cucumbers and onions into separate bowls. Sprinkle salt over sliced cucumbers. Cover with ice cubes; let stand several hours to chill cucumbers. Replace ice if necessary. Drain well. Add onions to cucumbers. Put all remaining ingredients into large kettle. Bring to a boil and boil hard for 10 minutes. Add cucumbers and onion slices, return to a boil, and boil hard for 10 minutes. Pack in hot pint jars (500 ml each). Adjust caps. Process in a boiling water bath canner for 30 minutes.

8 pints (4 liters)

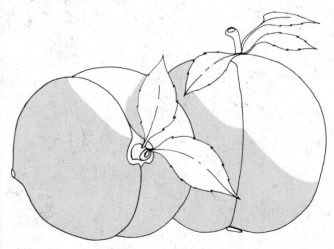

Apple Chutney, Pear Honey (page 161), Raw Cranberry Relish (page 166)

Carrot Pickles

Pickled carrot slices are a colorful accompaniment to meat.

>   2 or 3 bunches small carrots
>   1 cup (250 ml) sugar
>   2 cups (500 ml) vinegar
> 1 1/2 cups (375 ml) water
>   1 teaspoon (5 ml) salt
>   1 tablespoon (15 ml) mixed
>   pickling spices
>   1 stick cinnamon

Prepare jars and lids for canning. Pare carrots. Assemble Salad Maker with Crinkle Cut or Thick Slicer Disc and large bowl. Process carrots. Cook carrots until just tender; drain. Combine sugar, vinegar, water and salt in saucepan. Tie spices in cheesecloth bag; add to vinegar mixture. Boil 5 to 8 minutes. Pack carrots into hot pint (500 ml) jars, leaving 1/4-inch (0.6 cm) head space. Discard spice bag. Heat syrup to boiling. Carefully pour syrup, boiling hot, over carrots, leaving 1/4-inch (0.6 cm) head space. Adjust caps. Process in boiling water bath canner for 30 minutes. Remove jars and let cool on racks.

About 3 pints (1.5 liters)

Raw Cranberry Relish

Serve at room temperature or chilled.

>   4 cups (1 liter) cranberries
>   1 large orange, cut in eighths
>   2 cups (500 ml) sugar

Assemble Food Grinder with Coarse Disc. Grind cranberries and orange into small mixer bowl. Add sugar and stir well. Cover and allow to stand at room temperature about 1 hour before serving.

4 cups (1 liter)

Canned Apple Juice

Follow this procedure to can as much apple juice as you wish.

>   3 pounds (1.5 kg) apples
>   (approximately) per pint

Wash apples thoroughly and remove stem and blossom ends. Cut in half. Assemble Juice Extractor. Process apples at recommended speed. Bring apple juice just to a boil in large saucepan. Skim off foam. Pour into hot canning jars leaving 1/4-inch (0.6 cm) head space. Adjust caps. Process pints (500 ml) or quarts (liters) for 10 minutes in boiling water bath canner. Remove jars and let cool on racks.

Note: A clearer juice can be produced by filtering through cheesecloth before heating.

16 servings

Canned Apples for Pies

>   8 pounds (4 kg) apples, cored
>   and pared
>   1 cup (250 ml) sugar
>   4 cups (1 liter) water

Prepare jars and lids for canning. Measure sugar and water into a saucepan; cook until sugar dissolves. Keep syrup hot until needed, but do not let boil down. Assemble Salad Maker with Thick Slicer Disc. Process apples. To prevent darkening, place sliced apples in a solution of 8 cups water (2 liters) and 4 teaspoons (20 ml) commercial ascorbic acid mixture. Drain apples, boil in syrup 5 minutes. Carefully pack, hot, into pint (500 ml) jars leaving 1/2-inch (1.3 cm) head space. Remove air bubbles with a non-metallic kitchen utensil. Adjust caps. Process in boiling water bath canner for 20 minutes.

6 pints (3 liters)

Love In A Small Jar

Sometimes great convenience comes in small containers. Oster "Mini-Blend" containers allow you to purée foods in small amounts for your infant or toddler, and refrigerate in the same container. So you not only know exactly what you're feeding your child, but you also enjoy the same convenience of commercial baby food. You can vary the basic purée ingredients and adjust the consistency from perfect smoothness to some chunkiness when your baby is ready for new tastes.

Then comes a variety of coffees that can make your next coffee-klatch the talk of the neighborhood. There is Café Bavarian Mint, Café Suisse Mocha just for starters.

"Mini-Blend" container convenience comes to the rescue, too, with Butterscotch Sauce and Exotic Seasoning. Why not show your love for friends by giving them a "Mini-Blend" container filled with one of these recipes!

Café Bavarian Mint

A candy bar to drink, thanks to Mini-Blend ease!.

- 1/4 cup (50 ml) powdered non-dairy creamer
- 1/3 cup (75 ml) granulated sugar
- 1/4 cup (50 ml) instant coffee
- 2 tablespoons (30 ml) powdered baking cocoa
- 2 hard candy peppermints, broken into several pieces

Put all ingredients into Mini-Blend container. Process at LIQUEFY until blended. Use 1 level tablespoon of mixture with 6-ounces (200 ml) boiling water for each cup. Stir well. If desired, serve with a dollop of whipped cream. For extra mint flavor, serve with a peppermint stick.

14 6-ounce (200 ml each) servings

Meat Combo Dish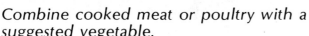

Combine cooked meat or poultry with a suggested vegetable.

 1/2 **cup (125 ml) cubed cooked lamb, beef, veal, or chicken**
 2 **tablespoons (30 ml) cooked vegetables (carrots, peas, spinach, celery, squash)**
 1 **slice bacon, crisp-fried**
 1/2 **cup (125 ml) milk**
 1/4 **cup (50 ml) cooked rice**

Assemble Blender. Put all ingredients into blender container. Cover and process at BLEND until thoroughly puréed. Heat before serving.

2 or 3 servings

Basic Puréed Meat or Vegetable

Thin cooked meat or vegetables with liquid as suggested.

 1/2 **cup (125 ml) cubed cooked meat or vegetable**
 4 **to 6 tablespoons (60 to 90 ml) milk, formula, or other liquid**

Put ingredients into "Mini-Blend" container and process at PUREE until smooth. To test for smoothness, rub a small amount between your fingers. If any large particles can be felt, continue processing. (Add full amount of liquid for very young babies; decrease amount as child grows older.)

3/4 cup (200 ml)

Basic Puréed Canned or Fresh Fruit

Drain canned fruit or cooked fresh fruit before measuring and puréeing with liquid.

 3/4 **cup (200 ml) cooked fruit**
 2 **teaspoons (10 ml) fruit juice or water**

Put ingredients into "Mini-Blend" container and process at PUREE until smooth. To test for smoothness, rub a small amount between your fingers. If any large particles can be felt, continue processing. (Add full amount of liquid for very young babies; decrease amount as child grows older.)

3/4 cup (200 ml)

Café Suisse Mocha

Delight the bridge group with Chocolate Quick Cake (page 140) and this complementary coffee.

 1/4 **cup (50 ml) powdered non-dairy coffee creamer**
 1/3 **cup (75 ml) granulated sugar**
 1/4 **cup (50 ml) instant coffee**
 2 **tablespoons (30 ml) powered baking cocoa**

Put all ingredients into "Mini-Blend" container and process at LIQUEFY until well blended. Use 1 level tablespoon (15 ml) of mixture with 6 ounces (200 ml) boiling water for each cup. Stir well. If desired, serve with a dollop of whipped cream.

14 6-ounce (200 ml each) servings

Basic Pureed Canned or Fresh Fruit, Basic Pureed Meat or Vegetable, Meat Combo Dish

Café Cappuccino

Just right for the fireside with that special person in your life.

- 1/3 cup (75 ml) powdered non-dairy creamer
- 1/3 cup (75 ml) sugar
- 1/4 cup (50 ml) instant coffee
- 1 orange flavored hard candy

Put all ingredients into "Mini-Blend" container. Process at LIQUEFY until well blended. Use 1 level tablespoon (15 ml) of mixture with 6 ounces (200 ml) boiling water for each cup. Stir well. Garnish with a dollop of whipped cream or a slice of orange, if desired.

14 6-ounce (200 ml each) servings

Café Viennese

Keep all four of our special coffees on hand for a quick energy boost whenever you need it.

- 1/4 cup (50 ml) powdered non-dairy creamer
- 1/3 cup (75 ml) granulated sugar
- 1/4 cup (50 ml) instant coffee
- 1/2 teaspoon (2 ml) ground cinnamon

Put all ingredients into "Mini-Blend" container. Process at LIQUEFY until well blended. Use 1 level tablespoon (15 ml) of mixture with 6 ounces (200 ml) boiling water for each cup. For extra flavor, serve with a cinnamon swizzle stick, or garnish with a dollop of whipped cream.

14 6-ounce (200 ml each) servings

Butterscotch-Brandy Sauce

Got a minute? The kids would love an ice cream treat with this sauce.

- 1/2 cup (125 ml) butterscotch chips
- 2 tablespoons (30 ml) butter or margarine
- 1 teaspoon (5 ml) brandy extract
- 1/4 cup (50 ml) hot milk

Put all ingredients into "Mini-Blend" container. Process at BLEND until smooth.

about 3/4 cup (200 ml)

Exotic Seasoning

Wow, what a twist! Friends will love some to take home.

- 2 tablespoons (30 ml) black peppercorns
- 2 tablespoons (30 ml) coriander seeds
- 1 1/2 tablespoons (22 ml) caraway seeds
- 1 stick of cinnamon
- 1 tablespoon (15 ml) whole cloves
- 1 tablespoon (15 ml) cardamom seeds
- 1 piece of whole ginger
- 2 tablespoons (30 ml) garlic chips
- 1 tablespoon (15 ml) mustard seeds

Put all ingredients into "Mini-Blend" container. Process at GRIND until blended. Add to stews and casserole dishes during cooking. Sprinkle on squash, pumpkin, just before serving.

3/4 cup (200 ml)

INDEX

The Oster Kitchen Center® Cookbook